Making Your
Dreams Come True®

MARCIA WIEDER

America's Dream Coach

HARMONY BOOKS / New York

Published by Harmony Books, 201 East 50th Street, New York, New York 10022. Member of the Crown Publishing Group.
Random House, Inc. New York, Toronto, London, Sydney, Auckland
www.randomhouse.com

Originally published, in different form, by Greater Wisdom Publishing Corporation in 1993.

HARMONY BOOKS is a registered trademark and Harmony Books colophon is a trademark of Random House, Inc.

MAKING YOUR DREAMS COME TRUE is a registered trademark of Marcia Wieder.

Printed in the United States of America

Design by Cindy LaBreacht

Library of Congress Cataloging-in-Publication Data
Wieder, Marcia.
    Making your dreams come true / by Marcia Wieder. Rev. ed.
        1. Success—Psychological aspects. I. Title.
    BF637.S8W512 1999
        158.1—dc21   99-31657
    ISBN 0-609-60608-5

10 9 8 7 6 5 4 3 2 1

First Revised Edition

For all who dare to dream—

I recognize and honor the dreamer you are.

Acknowledgments

THANK YOU TO MY FAMILY and dear friends who love and support me and believe in my dreams. You are my core.

Thank you, Bonnie Solow, for bringing me to our amazing DreamTeam at Random House. I am honored to have partners who can dream bigger than I can, especially Patricia Gift.

Thank you, Lori Glasgow and Jan Tilmon at KVIE Public Broadcasting, and Lori Lane, for daring to dream big and for committing to our television show because you believed it was the right message at the right time and that I was the right voice. And thank you to Caroll Roberson. Your intention and conviction helped make some of my dreams happen.

Mostly, thank *you* for reading this book and for spreading the word that our dreams are precious and essential. May your life be filled with love, joy, and dreams come true.

And thank you, God, for reminding me that we are all dreamers at heart, and for granting me the privilege of doing this work.

Contents

Foreword

WHAT IF YOU COULD CREATE what you want by closing the gap between dreams and reality? In person and now in *Making Your Dreams Come True,* Marcia Wieder shows people how to do just that.

In her work as a professional speaker, Marcia's spirit and style electrifies any room. She produces powerful results with her corporate clients and business associates worldwide. After engaging with Marcia, people who claim to have forgotten their dreams remember and get going on them.

I first met Marcia shortly after reading books by Richard Bach and Jane Roberts. These writings profoundly changed my life, and when I realized they could change others' lives too, I felt compelled to share this joy with everyone I came in contact with. Just then, I met Marcia. This was coincidence #1.

Our career paths took us in different directions, and we lost contact for some time. At the precise moment when I was rediscovering my own true purpose and my life was beginning to move in an exciting new direction, Marcia called me and asked me to read *Making Your Dreams Come True* and write a foreword. I felt the joy of the knowledge and wisdom contained in this book, and again the compulsion to help share it with everyone. Coincidence #2.

It is said that when the student is ready, the teacher will appear and vice versa. The fact that you are reading this book is no accident. Coincidence #3.

Marianne Williamson writes that all of our choices are made either out of love or out of fear. *Making Your Dreams Come True* also speaks to this basic truth. If you are passionate, love what you do, and spread that love through what you do, the possibilities are limitless.

There are many paths to the truth. In this book, Marcia has garnered truths from numerous sources and has uniquely combined this knowledge in a practical and pragmatic guide to self-discovery or, better yet, rediscovery. This book provides a real basis for applying these truths, and gives us an imaginative action plan that starts us on a path toward the realization of our greatest dreams.

I have rediscovered that I am happiest and most successful when working with the things I love, that are exciting to me, that I feel passionate about, and in which I feel a need to make a contribution. Through all my various career experiences, from being NBC's executive in charge of the original *Saturday Night Live* to becoming an Emmy-winning producer, I have always been most successful when surrounded by, or in close proximity to, the objects of my passion.

With regard to all the coincidences, the explanation "it's a coincidence" doesn't really explain anything. A coincidence is merely two or more events coinciding, the odds of which are very highly improbable if not impossible. The power of dreams and the power you will derive from *Making Your Dreams Come True* will allow you to transcend the improbable and the impossible. Read the book . . . and then count the coincidences!

—Rick Traum, Producer

Preface

**You've got to have a dream
if you want to make a dream come true.**

YOU ARE ABOUT TO EMBARK on an exciting personal journey in a realm that you perhaps thought you couldn't do much about—making your dreams come true. Bring along your doubts, fears, and concerns and I will help you address them head on. But also bring your hopes and highest aspirations, because *Making Your Dreams Come True* is going to show you how to make them part of your everyday existence.

My life is a dream come true. In all areas of my life, I'm living a life I love. This book will show you how to do the same for yourself.

This is a tried-and-true, tested and proven program that will take you through a step-by-step process for making all your dreams come true.

Here is the basic formula:

1. Get clear about what your dream is.
2. Remove the obstacles, especially the limiting beliefs.
3. Design the simple steps to make your dream happen.

The essence of the formula is passion. Passion excites and compels you. It makes your life rich and extraordinary. This book will show you how to discover or rediscover what you're passionate about and how to bring it to all areas of your life. How does that sound?

For ten years I lived in Washington, D.C., and was president of a multimedia creative services agency managing up to fourteen employees. Although successful by many people's standards, I was not passionate about what I was doing, about how I was doing it, about the people with whom I was doing it, or about where I was doing it.

My dream was to be free—free to travel anywhere at any time. Free to do what I wanted when I wanted, even to have a portable office wherever I happened to be.

My dream included a magnificent view of water and mountains, clean fresh air, and a quiet, healthy environment.

My dream included partnering with creative visionaries to make an impact on the world, in addition to traveling the world in style and elegance, speaking about something inspiring.

My dream included having lots of fun, creating my work as play, and living a life filled with self-expression.

Sound outrageous?

I picked up and moved to San Francisco. When people ask why, I tell them because I was craving a beautiful view and a different lifestyle, which is what matters to me now. Once committed, I climbed into my car and took a few months to visit with friends and family as I made my way west, with my fax machine and portable computer in tow.

Since then I've become a successful dream coach, speaker, and author. During the past few months, I have been paid to travel to Hawaii, Rome, Greece, and Indonesia to inspire people to dream.

I've worked with thousands of people personally and professionally in some of the biggest and most wonderful companies in the world. I help them get clear about their vision and mission, and I support them as they get into action on their dreams and their lives. I founded and lead Dream University®, a weeklong retreat for visionaries and big dreamers, which I hold at exotic resorts and spas worldwide. I look and feel ten years younger, and I'm the healthiest I've ever been. I'm completely free and very happy.

It all begins with a dream. You can make your dreams come true. It all starts here. So let's begin finding, fine-tuning, and achieving your dreams.

MAKING YOUR DREAMS COME TRUE

Introduction

A new consulting business of dream architects
to help people implement their dreams will show up.

—FAITH POPCORN, *THE POPCORN REPORT*

YOU ARE HOLDING IN YOUR HANDS the definitive work on
making your dreams come true, having the life you love, and living with passion—in essence, having it all. When you finish reading this book you will know:

> ➤ What you really want your life to be like.
> ➤ How to develop a dream that inspires you.
> ➤ How to look at your life from a fresh perspective.
> ➤ How to design your environment to implement the tech-
>   niques you've learned.

Beginning with the first chapter you will learn to empower yourself and believe in your ideas. Possibilities you never knew existed
will emerge, and you will trust your resources to help you produce
amazing results with greater ease in your everyday life.

Sound enticing?

In every chapter you will find clarity as well as the action
steps that will prompt you to nod in knowing appreciation. The
pages in this book will offer you methods of achieving everything

1

you want in life. The hands-on exercises presented throughout will serve as your personal record of everything you learned about your dreams and how to realize them. The Making Your Dreams Come True Workbook will walk you through the process.

This book is written with you as its focus. You can pretend it is a highly paid dream coach or architect, leading you by the hand through the process of making your dreams come true. Interact fully with it, and when you are done, I believe you'll say, "Yes, I can make my dreams come true anytime I choose."

A wonderful dream story accompanies the publication of this book. It demonstrates exactly what I teach. You need to believe in your dream, even if it initially seems like a long shot. Find DreamTeam members who will support you and help make your dream happen. Eventually, as you articulate your dream with passion and clarity, and demonstrate that you believe in your dream, others will get on board and perhaps even take your dream to a much higher level.

Years ago I had the pleasure of meeting George Hall, vice president for Body Wise International, a wonderful network marketing company that sells nutritional supplements and believes in personal empowerment. George and I had an immediate affinity for each other, since we are both big dreamers. As a matter of fact, George is six feet six and a stunt pilot enthusiast. One of his dreams was to compete in aerobatic flying, which he later did. George hired me to speak at several events for Body Wise, to inspire thousands of people to take risks and go for their dreams.

One of the people in the audience was Caroll Roberson. Caroll later attended Dream University® (you'll read more about her story) and so believed in my message that she came back as a facilitator. Caroll became an essential member of my DreamTeam. Here's what happened.

I made a substantial investment to produce an audiotape series called *Yes You Can . . . Make Your Dreams Real.* Caroll sent the tapes to her friend Lori Glasgow at KVIE Public Broadcasting System in Sacramento, California. But Caroll didn't stop there. She was tenacious and relentless in urging Lori to listen to the tapes. Lori listened, loved my message, and called me. She wanted to feature me in a one-hour national television special and invited me to become a partner. The magic had begun.

Then I met Jan Tilmon, a creative and brilliant woman at KVIE who helped launch the careers of two wonderful writers, Leo Buscaglia and Covert Bailey *(Fit or Fat)*. Her vision was that my life was about to change for the better, as people worldwide would soon hear my message. We agreed that we would produce a show called *Making Your Dreams Come True* and I would travel all over the United States as part of a major fund-raising drive for PBS.

There was just one thing missing. In conjunction with the audiotapes, we needed a book. We literally had only six months to get it into the stores, and we had not identified a publisher for it. I called my agent, Bonnie Solow. She was concerned about the time frame, but my passion ignited her, and she made an important phone call to a woman of true vision, a really big dreamer. Patty Gift at Random House asked me to rush her my materials, and in less than twenty-four hours we had an amazing deal and a commitment to put this book into the stores and into your hands right away.

As luck would have it, I was flying to New York the next day to present a workshop to The Gap. I swung by Random House and met my new team. It was amazing. The entire team was there to greet and welcome me: Chip Gibson, the publisher; Patty Gift, my new editor and immediate friend; Andy Martin, the associate publisher; Tina Constable and Emily Hannon from publicity; Cheri De

Luca from foreign rights; Alison Gross from marketing; and Kristen Wolfe, the editorial assistant.

I left this meeting filled with joy. I had found the perfect DreamTeam. They passed the true test of a great DreamTeam with flying colors: they love my dream, they are willing and able to make my dream theirs, and finally—and this is my favorite part—they will make my dream even bigger.

Everyone you meet serves an important role in your life. Use this book to sharpen your awareness and to find like-minded big dreamers. Through this very special book, reconnect to your passion, find and create dreams that honor your heart's desire, and prepare for the magic and surprises that are available to all dreamers. Count me as a member of your DreamTeam.

CHAPTER 1

What Is a Dream?

Nothing happens unless first a dream.

—CARL SANDBURG

MOST PEOPLE THINK OF DREAMS either as some unattainable fantasies or as something they do in their sleep. Neither definition is what I mean when I speak of dreams.

I define dreams as the aspirations, desires, goals, and hopes that you most want for yourself. These are the dreams you have while you are wide awake.

Here is my formula for making your dreams come true:

FIRST
Get clear about what your dream is.

SECOND
Remove the obstacles, especially the limiting beliefs.

THIRD
Design the simple steps to make your dream happen.

It's that simple. That's the formula for having it all—a life you love, and the time and freedom to enjoy it.

THREE KEY WORDS

The word "dreams" has long been misinterpreted, as if dreams were like puffy clouds in the sky—beautiful but unreachable. The dictionary offers a different interpretation not only of "dreams" but of several other words that I'll be using throughout this process. I'll start by defining some terms:

dream A fond hope or aspiration; to conceive of or devise

possibility That which may or can be; that which may or can be done; that which is capable of existing; something that is conceivable

beliefs What you hold to be true; your opinions and judgments

It's interesting that the dictionary defines "dream" as a fond aspiration which suggests possibility and hope, while most people have a sense of hopelessness and futility about their dreams. Yet their dreams continue to live, like embers glowing in the back of their minds. Using this book, you will learn to be clear about what you want, and to get your dreams out of your head and into your reality.

Many of us regard "possibility" as something that's not *impossible*, although Webster tells us that a possibility is something that is within our grasp. I used to believe that anything was possible as long as I could figure out in advance how to do it. Eventually I realized this was a limiting belief because sometimes the perfect strategy might not be immediately evident. Not having a plan all mapped out should not be the reason you don't believe something might happen. I was stopping myself from going for what I wanted, often before I even began. Now I know that *everything is possible* as long as I believe it. Believing in our dreams often gives us the courage to act on them, to take the important steps forward. My life is filled with opportunities galore, many that I surely would not have encountered if I were still operating with my old belief.

Indeed, when you open up to the potential of having what you want, you allow wonderful people and events to appear in your life. When you clarify what you're committed to having, and when you believe that everything is possible, the results in your life will seem effortless and show up easily. Do you want greater ease in your life?

I love the dictionary definition of "possibility." It reinforces the concept that much of our lives can be filled with extraordinary results. Have you written this off as illusionary? Are you overly realistic? Reality is an important part of the mix, but being too realistic can squelch your passion and your dreams.

Dreams belong in our homes and in the workplace. In the ideal situation, which I'll discuss in detail, you will bring more of what you love into your everyday life. Take Paul Scott, the senior vice president of Worldwide Field Operations at Lucent Technologies, for example. Paul has a passion for fun, which he demonstrates every day at work, even in times of change and pressure. Since one of his true passions is golf, he's always willing to entertain and educate important clients out on a beautiful course. And why not? He totally gets it about passion as does his exceptional and cutting-edge company. Lucent Technologies hired me to design and implement a yearlong program called the Passion Plan. They know that happy people make happy employees, and happy employees produce better results.

AT&T, one of America's corporate giants, had a campaign for its employees called Ten Million Magic Moments. AT&T said, and I agree, that it's time to find a new way of thinking, doing, and speaking about things, which includes fun and creativity. Whether we refer to it as purpose or mission, there is an important place for vision in business, too. The mission statement of Charles Schwab, the financial giant, says, "We are the custodian of our customers' financial dreams." That's why Schwab has my business.

You can start making your personal and professional dreams come true today—right now—by being clear about what a dream is, by believing in your dreams, and by taking a few simple steps.

WHAT IS YOUR DREAM?

When I listen to people as they discuss their dreams, they seem so quickly to abandon what they want. They often say something like this: "Well, it might be nice, but it will probably never happen, so why bother?" Are you simply dismissing your most heartfelt desires? Do you even know what they are?

In talking to people about what they want, I find that most of them regard dreams in the same way they perceive fantasies. They don't believe their dreams will come true unless something miraculous happens: they win the lottery, Mr. or Ms. Right comes along, or their stars are aligned in the heavens.

Here is a simple and powerful distinction between a dream and a fantasy. In a dream you can design a strategy for making it happen. In a fantasy like winning the lottery, there is nothing that you can do to make sure it happens. Sure, fantasies can occur, but again, there is nothing you or I can do to ensure it.

Keep in mind that you are the one who needs to make the distinction. When I announced to friends and family that I was moving to San Francisco to become a dream coach, they thought this was a fantasy and were concerned about my sanity. But I believed in my dream, I could conceive of the strategy, and was committed to making it happen. In other words, it was a dream, and it did come true.

Everything Is Possible.

A dream can be exotic or glamorous, but it does not have to be. Your dream can be anything from spending more time with the family to growing your business. It can be to become healthier and more physically fit, or to write a book. Dreams can range from the mundane to the esoteric, and sometimes what you truly want can come as a complete surprise to you. At the end of this chapter you will find some Real People stories. These anecdotes are used as illustrations throughout the book. They are all true situations and they all demonstrate how the techniques I'll describe can be used in every facet of your life.

LIFE CAN BE

A DREAM COME TRUE.

To enter into the process of achieving your dream, start with step one: clarifying what you want. On page 10 there is a place for you to commit your dream to paper. Put into a single sentence the essence of what you're committed to having. Don't worry that you can't envision all the details; they'll materialize as you move forward. The key is to get in touch with what you feel passionate about, what excites and motivates you. If you don't know what your dream is and if that is the main reason why you bought this book, I have two simple suggestions. You could write, "My dream is to have a dream" (trust me, you are not alone on this one), or you could start small, by writing down one small thing that you would like to have or do. Remember, a dream is simply something you want.

Write down what you want. If you can't formulate your dream yet, make something up. Start someplace. Although it may seem ridiculous now, it will often work to lead you down the right path. When you're ready to write your dream, you can apply the techniques you learn as you move through this book. Think about a time in your life when you spoke to others about an idea, and your idea turned into something concrete. Perhaps the more you talked about your concept, the more real it became. By getting your dream out of your head, you will get the ball rolling.

IDENTIFYING YOUR DREAM

Example: I, Diane, will have great success in my new business while balancing my family and social life. (Balance, in some form, is the most common dream people have mentioned to me.)

I, _____, have the following dream:

_____

_____

_____

WHAT ARE YOUR EXPECTATIONS?

What do you expect to have when you've finished this book? Perhaps you're looking for a blueprint to get you from where you are to where you want to be. Maybe you're seeking a strategy or steps that will divide the work of reaching your dreams into specific areas of concentration.

You can turn this book into an action plan for making your dreams come true by deciding now what you intend to have by the time you've finished reading it. My goal is that you fulfill your dreams as you complete the book; if that's not your goal too, you may want to put the book down now and think about why you bought it in the first place.

The process of defining your expectations and getting your dream out of your head and into reality can follow these steps:

Think about what you want.
Visualize what you want.
Write down what you want and read it aloud to yourself.
Speak with others about what you want.
Look for opportunities to make your dreams come true.
Live as though your dream has already come true.
Do what you want to do, so that you can have what you want to have.
Get up and get going. As Nike says, "Just do it."

Start to act the part right now. If your dream is to run a dude ranch, the first thing you might do is buy boots and a cowboy hat and have fun wearing them around the house. I know it's a small step, and to your rational mind it may even seem a little silly, but you have to start wherever you can. This becomes your point of access or port of entry. Besides, if your dream is to play golf in the Masters Tournament, you have to get out there and practice.

That first step may be enough for you right now. Perhaps you decide that you want to be in greater action toward your dream, or that you want your dream to come true in its entirety by the end of this book. It's all up to you. Have a sense of humor and play with it; it doesn't need to be hard work. Enjoy the process.

The techniques await you. Don't sit back to see how it unfolds; your dream *won't* happen unless you interact with the process. Let this book make a difference in your life; use it to pull you forward so you can get what you want. Start now.

MY GOAL IS TO HELP YOU

FULFILL YOUR DREAMS

AS YOU COMPLETE THIS BOOK.

Real People: LARRY

Larry wanted to double his business within the next calendar year without burning himself out. His goal was reasonable; in fact, it's done all the time. Larry came to me because he didn't know how to accomplish that goal and he felt that something was in his way. He couldn't quite put his finger on what the obstacle was.

I told Larry that we'd start the process of making his dream come true by getting in touch with what he's passionate about. Larry balked. "Wait a minute," he said. "I don't want to examine my whole life. I just want to know how to double my business."

I said, "Larry, you have to trust the process." He'd heard these words before.

What Larry discovered by following my approach was that powerful partnerships and intimate relationships had been a driving force throughout his life; that was what excited him. He knew this subconsciously, but articulating it gave him a real boost of energy. He was excited about making this realization a part of his business goal.

When he realized the passion he felt about creating powerful partnerships, Larry understood that he needed to learn how to develop associations with anyone at any time and that this would be the secret to his success.

As we continued to probe, Larry became aware that, by holding on to old beliefs that no longer served his needs, he was limiting his ability to create partnerships. For example, he had developed the habit of not revealing his playing cards, he feared taking the wrong kind of people into his confidence, and he worried that others wouldn't uphold their end of a bargain or that they didn't have the right address or the best credentials to be his partner. He eliminated some wonderful potential partners without ever giving them a chance. Together we removed these obstacles, the limiting beliefs that were in Larry's way. This had a huge impact and immediately freed him up to dream big.

Once he was clear about what made him feel passionate and with his limiting beliefs out of the way, Larry made a conscious commitment to develop partnerships with anyone he chose. Now he's excited about living his life, not just about doubling his business.

Passion provides access to power; when Larry got in touch with his passion, he developed the power to take the first step toward his dream. Now he has more than two dozen strategic partnerships with associates, friends, agents, even competitors, all of whom are helping him achieve his goal. Larry now understands that passion is a component in the formula for success and that people are central to his passion.

Trust the process

of making your dreams come true.

Real People: NANCY

Nancy had been successful on Wall Street, making a six-figure salary. Now she was starting a whole new life: she was pregnant with her first child, and she was leaving the world of stocks and bonds to start her own business. She was absolutely committed to her dream of spending quality personal time with her friends and family, while developing and building a new business. She was determined to lead a balanced life.

A successful person is often also an overcommitted person, and Nancy fit that description. She was aware that she had built so much into her life that there wasn't room to create anything new. We began, therefore, by cleaning out the clutter. We moved things out of the way, consolidated, organized, and created space, not just physically but emotionally, mentally, and spiritually. Finally, Nancy had *room* to design a whole new future, and she began to live her dream by making deliberate choices, not merely responding to whatever life threw her way.

Then we designed the strategies for her to achieve her dream. There were specific marketing and sales techniques for growing the business, but there were also strategies for enjoying her pregnancy and having quality time with her husband.

Wherever possible we doubled up on strategies to allow Nancy more personal time. One tactic was for Nancy and her husband to take a daily walk together. We later turned this technique into a project with the goal of walking two hundred miles before the baby was born. This supported Nancy's need for a healthy body and baby, for exercise and relaxation, and for time with her spouse. Do you need to clear away clutter in order to make some serious space for your dreams? You'll learn more about projects, strategies, and steps as you read on.

Get in touch with your passion.

Real People: ILENE

Ilene was once a professional dancer who had studied with Alvin Ailey. She founded a small dance company as a sideline while working at a full-time job. Her dream was to quit her job, to become the full-time executive director of her dance company, and to do it within thirty days.

She had many beliefs and fears that were stopping her from achieving her dream. Ilene and I worked intensely through a long session to get clear about her dream and to remove the self-imposed limits that prevented her from reaching it. As we grappled with these issues, she began to talk about her dream, expressing her hope of making it happen. She was committed to finding people who would help her. Ilene was surprised and delighted to find that going through the process made her see the dream as bigger than her current reality; this change of perception made her more committed to realizing her dream than to remaining in the status quo.

Live your dream by making deliberate choices rather that just responding to whatever life throws your way.

One of Ilene's concerns had been how she would finance her new venture and support herself at the same time. Together we were able to devise a plan that enabled her to resign from her full-time position and still pay her bills. We did that by finding a skill—grant-proposal writing—that Ilene could use as a free-lancer. Once she realized she didn't need to be a salaried employee, she turned her current employer into her client, and she earned $10,000 in the first few weeks of freelancing. Originally Ilene had thought that her employer would not support her dream. This was a limiting belief that she uncovered and removed.

Once Ilene knew how she would pay the rent, she turned her attention to her new venture. She assembled a board, scheduled recitals, and got into action living her dream. She did not have the budget to fulfill this dream, but her passion, commitment, and hard work—known as sweat equity—made it happen. The first major performance of Ilene's dance company, which I'm pleased to say I attended, was offered to an audience of more than two hundred people.

Commit to your dream.

Real People: GEORGE

At one time George had been severely overweight. Through great effort and perseverance, he had trimmed down and was feeling great about being healthy. Now his dream was to stay physically fit, but he was having trouble getting motivated to go to the gym three times a week.

In exploring George's life we discovered that his passion was to live life as an adventure. To George, that meant trying new things and seeking new challenges. In short, George hated feeling bored.

Out of his enthusiasm for testing himself in new situations, George designed a project that would allow him to fulfill his dream adventurously. The project he took on was to train for a triathlon. The venture had George feeling turned on, lit up, and passionate, and he had no difficulty getting to the gym regularly. He even hired a coach to help him. The more George pushed himself beyond where he was, the more passionate he became. This is inherent in his purpose: to live life as an adventure.

Here's a quick note for you: If your dream is to be in great shape without having to go to the gym, this need not be considered a fantasy. My strategy for exercising without daily visits to the gym included taking up skiing and in-line skating (with lots of appropriate padding) at the age of forty.

Make your dream bigger

than your current reality.

Real People: THE CARTERS

The Carters owned a computer store in an upscale shopping center. Like many people, their dream was to have financial freedom while having the time to enjoy each other. After a session with me, the Carters realized that maintaining their current business was working against achieving their dream. The massive overhead in their expensive setting was eroding their profits, and the retail nature of their establishment meant that they were always on call when the store was open. They needed more flexibility, and they recognized that, to get it, they would have to close the store and establish another business. They considered this a daring and a very scary move.

Allow yourself to get lit up,

turned on,

and really passionate

about your dream.

One of the advantages of the techniques in this book is that they can be used to create balance; after all, part of having it all is having the time to enjoy it. The Carters didn't know at first that their dream included closing down their store; that only became clear during the process. They were passionate both about being in business and about having time for each other, but their passion did not include owning a retail operation. Once they were committed to realizing their passion, they were ready to get into action toward having their dream. You will see as their story continues later in this book that they did it in record time.

CHAPTER 2

The Passion Pyramid

Passion provides access to power.

—MARCIA WIEDER

MY TECHNIQUES FOR MAKING your dreams come true have several advantages over other approaches. One of the benefits is that you don't have to choose between having your dream in one area of your life and getting what you want in other areas.

I often hear people lament that they could have what they want if they gave up other things, or that they must work endless, tedious hours to earn the kind of money they need. I don't believe it's necessary to make sacrifices like these to have your dream—that is, it's not necessary to forfeit anything you want, providing you are clear about your dreams.

When you are passionate, you are focused, purposeful, and determined. Your body, mind, and heart are all moving in unison toward the same goal. Richard Bach, in *The Bridge Across Forever*, tells us that when we are "passionately obsessed by anything we love—sailboats, airplanes, ideas—an avalanche of magic flattens the way ahead, levels rules, reasons, deserts, bears us with it over chasms, fears, doubts."

Passionate thinking is a driving ambition. It comes from a

place within you that provides emotional reinforcement. This energy is what you want to harness in propelling your dreams into reality, and I designed the Passion Pyramid to help you do it.

The Passion Pyramid is a tool. It will help you see how to get from where you are to where you want to be while keeping you balanced in all the areas of your life. It is designed to help you bring into your life more of what matters to you and what you love, at work and at home every day. As you strive to make your dreams come true, the information you put into the pyramid is the foundation on which everything else rests.

You will find a copy of the pyramid on page 22. Use it to align the four *p*'s that can ignite your dreams—purpose, passion, possibilities, and power. When used properly, the Passion Pyramid can help you design a blueprint for achieving what you want and for streamlining the process of realizing your dreams.

This pyramid is intended to be read and used from the bottom up. Most of us live our lives from the top down. Then something happens—a fire that needs to be put out or something to which you must attend. You look at your calendar (scheduling) to see when you can fit it in. Sometimes, if you're lucky, the activity may be related to a project you're working on or one you intend to start. If you're *very* lucky, the venture may even filter down into one of your dreams.

However, when you start working from the top down, whatever you're doing does not come from your purpose. You want to get to the top eventually, because that's where the rubber meets the road and where things actually get accomplished. To live a life that's filled with passion, you need to start with purpose and build up from the base. Let's look at how the sections of the Passion Pyramid show up in the world.

The Passion Pyramid

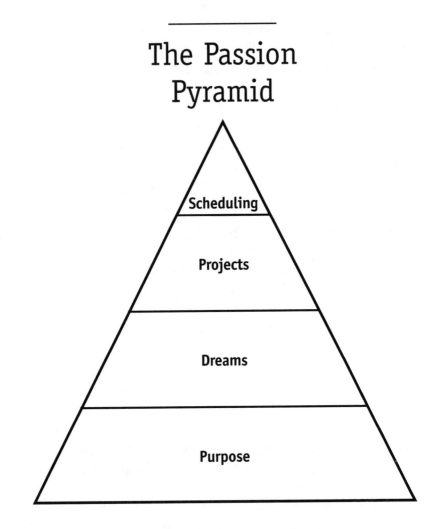

Scheduling

Projects

Dreams

Purpose

Once you have established your purpose,

you will be able to develop projects

that will take your dreams

out of your imagination

and make them part of your reality.

Purpose. Your purpose is the foundation; it answers the question "Who am I?" Some people think they've known the answer to that question for years. Then, like the captain in the Real People story at the end of this chapter, they are surprised to discover a different truth. Later we'll go through an exercise to answer the question "Who am I?"

Dreams. Once you have established your foundation and you know who you are, you can start to look at how you want your life to be. For example, if your purpose, like George's, is to live life as an adventure, your dreams might include bringing adventure into everything you do, or into a specific aspect of your life, like your business or your marriage. All of these are expressions of George's purpose, "To live life as an adventure." Larry's purpose, to live life in partnership, helped him to understand his dream of an extraordinarily close marriage and of powerful partnerships that generate profit. With clarity of purpose, your dreams develop a deeper meaning. This is so important.

Projects. Standing in your purpose, you will be able to develop projects that will take your dreams out of your imagination and make them part of your reality. Your projects will not only be real, but they will further the journey toward your dream by having built-in, specific, measurable results. Your projects are the means and measurement for accomplishing your dreams and making them real.

Scheduling. Scheduling, at the top of the pyramid, actually puts your projects onto the calendar, giving you dates by which to meet your objectives and make your dreams come true. The good news is that you will spend most of your time doing things you love, not just more busywork.

Having assembled the Passion Pyramid, three supporting elements now come into play: possibilities, power, and passion.

Possibilities: Looking at the possibilities in your life from the vantage point of your purpose, you will feel a new level of power and energy. You will see opportunities where you never saw them before, you will have a new appreciation of what you can make happen in your life, and you will allow yourself to remain open to new opportunities.

Power: The power to live your dreams every day stems from your ability to be "in action" on your dreams and to measure the specific results of your projects.

Passion: Standing figuratively and emotionally in your purpose, you will realize that passion permeates everything else. Your purpose is what compels you and kindles the passion to make your dreams come true.

Notice how the sections of the pyramid interconnect. Passion lives in all areas of your life, but it takes on special meaning as you bring it into your dreams; you can see possibilities from every vantage point on the Passion Pyramid, but they start to show up

The Passion Pyramid

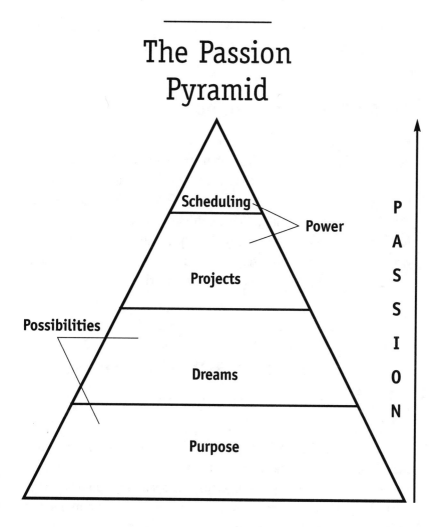

in ways you can recognize when you move from dreams to projects. The process is not linear; it is holographic and multidimensional.

MARCIA'S PASSION PYRAMID

My own purpose in life is to joyously self-express. How do I know? Because this is when I am the happiest and feel the most alive.

One of the highlights of my life was winning my eighth grade speech contest. I had such fun and spoke creatively about being the first woman astronaut. Once you meet me (which I hope will happen soon), you see instantly that "joyously self-expressing" is who I am. Memories of passionate moments in your life will help you find your purpose, as you will see shortly.

Passion permeates everything.

I believe in putting everything I want into my dreams. As I mentioned earlier, one dream that symbolizes my purpose is to travel the world in style and elegance, speaking publicly about something that will make a positive impact on people. So I decided to travel on a luxurious cruise ship as a guest speaker, offering workshops about making dreams come true. My project, one of any number I could have created, was a clear expression of my purpose—to joyously self-express—and an obvious representation of my dream. Because of the passion I felt, I knew that the project was completely consistent with my purpose.

Once the specific, measurable results of the project were defined, it was easy to get into action. As I gained clarity about what I wanted and created a project to achieve it, the big results easily happened. I spent the Christmas holidays cruising the Hawaiian Islands, all expenses paid for two.

Don't sabotage yourself by trying to deal with the Passion Pyramid from the top down. For example, most people have a negative reaction to "scheduling" because they feel anxious about finding time to take on additional tasks. Starting at the top of the pyramid rarely allows you to build a life you can live on purpose. Rest assured, however, that you will accomplish things faster and more easily when you are passionate and purposeful.

You can live the life that you love

filled with passion.

When I first started doing this work some years ago, I used to say, "Every day I'm doing something that I love." Now I can say, "I'm *always* doing things that I love." My office is devoid of files, except for project files. Since the projects come from my dreams, which come, in turn, from my purpose, I am living a life that I love, one that is filled with passion. Whenever I have extra time, which I often do, I reach for one of my project files. I love working on them because I know that doing so puts me constantly in action on the life I intentionally created for myself.

Real People: THE CAPTAIN

The captain had achieved what he thought was his life's dream. From the time he was seven years old he had dreamed of being a ship's captain. He held on to the dream for such a long time that, when he actually achieved it, he wondered, "Is this all there is?"

Passion was missing for him. He wasn't turned on by becoming captain; it was something he'd always thought he would do. After all, his father had been a captain, too.

What had initially been an empowering dream for the captain had become empty over the years. At age forty-five he found himself longing for the next twenty years to pass, so he could retire at sixty-five and move on to something else. He was appalled; what a terrible waste it would be to wait twenty years to be happy.

Passion provides access to power.

Gain access to your passion

through your life's purpose.

Then he started to realize that there was a different way to live his life, that he could have a new dream that would allow him to remain a sea captain while bringing passion into his life every day. He realized he had a talent for finding solutions to difficult problems, even dilemmas that others thought were impossible to resolve. He began to list his skills, and as he did so, he became aware that he was excited about some of them. He asked me to help him, and we began to turn his passion into projects.

When I last saw the captain, he was beginning to have conversations with engineering and trading companies, exploring the possibility of working with them when he wasn't at sea. The best news is that he was excited about potential new opportunities and enthusiastic about the new unpredictability of his life.

He laughed when he told me he had forgotten how much he liked surprises. He had allowed himself to fall into a rut, and until we got him moving toward his dream, he couldn't see how to get out.

Getting in touch with your passion will always get you out of your rut and onto a higher road. We'll discuss further how this can be done in Chapter 10.

Getting in touch with your passion

will always get you out of your rut

and onto a higher road.

CHAPTER 3

Remembering Your Purpose

The purpose of life is to live a life of purpose.
—ROBERT BYRNE

IF PASSION PROVIDES ACCESS TO POWER, the way to gain access to passion is through your life's purpose. Your purpose is to know who you are, what gets you excited; I might even say that your purpose is to remember why you're here. We are here to learn, to grow, and to express ourselves. And we all have great gifts and contributions to make as well.

A client once told me, "I made money and I was successful, but I still felt there must be something else."

"Yes, there's something else," I said. "It's called passion, and it comes from living your life on purpose."

If you're like a lot of readers, you might say, "I picked up this book because I wanted to make my dreams come true, but, between you and me, I don't think I have a purpose."

Yes, you do. Your purpose is not a big, burdensome, heavy weight that you must accomplish in your life; rather, it's an expression of who you are. Larry, who didn't think finding his purpose was the way to double his business, didn't increase sales until he defined who he was. After that, it was easy.

Your purpose could be anything that gets your juices flowing; it comes from what turns you on in life. The broader you state your purpose the better, because the broader your purpose the more room there is for passion and possibility. If you're concerned that your purpose is not going to be worthy enough or big enough or decent enough, here are some examples that others have offered when asked to complete the sentence, "My life's purpose is . . .":

To live life as an adventure
To create joy
To help others
To make a difference
To go beyond
To play and have fun (Yes, this too is a noble and worthy purpose.)

Your purpose is anything that touches your heart and makes a difference to you. If you're working at a job just for the money, and if what you're doing doesn't make you proud, perhaps you've lost your sense of purpose. The test is how you feel: are you turned on, or do you rationalize your work by saying that if you don't sell this product, somebody else will?

Most people are so busy filling the needs of daily life that they're happy just to get through the day. It's hard to live on purpose when life revolves around daily crises and you're always overwhelmed. By taking the time to define your purpose, you'll open up more time and space, have more energy, and be more focused. Then your life can change for the better.

Your purpose is who you are

and what gets you excited.

Your purpose is to remember why you're here.

DEFINING YOUR PURPOSE

You may wonder how to determine your purpose. Don't worry; you don't have to do it all at once, certainly not permanently and for all time. Life ebbs and flows, and your purpose may be modified accordingly over time.

When I first started speaking about my own purpose, I didn't describe it as "to joyously self-express." I began by looking at what I enjoyed doing. I liked to talk and travel, so I defined my life's purpose as "to talk and travel." Over time, that description was honed and sharpened, and yours will be, too; the more you work with it, the more it will start to resonate as a unique definition of who you are and who you are passionate about being.

Recently I watched a rerun of the movie *Fame*. Remember that scene when the keyboard player's father, the cabdriver, pulled up in front of the school, threw a huge speaker on the roof of his taxi, and started blaring his son's music? All the kids came running outside and started dancing wildly in the streets. This scene brought tears to my eyes, because here was what I love most—joyous self-expression.

You will eventually create a way to speak about your passion that really describes it for you. This is important. By completing the five-minute exercise on the next page, you will begin to get in touch with your life's purpose by reviewing a few of your special memories. One place to look for what turns you on is your past. What has excited you before? Don't think that your life is devoid of these experiences; everyone has them.

Your passionate memories may include graduating from college, meeting your spouse, getting a big raise. Or you may recall taking a special trip, having a baby, or accomplishing an important goal. If you can't find at least three memories of passion—I'm sure you've had at least thirty-three, maybe three hundred thirty-three—you're being too hard on yourself and setting your sights too high. Memorable moments come in all sizes.

It doesn't even matter if you harbor negative reactions to the memories, since anger and frustration can be mighty motivators. When you look back now, were you excited? Did you feel good? If you answer yes to those questions, write it down.

When you are done, take a deep breath and relax; the hard part is over. Now look for the pattern, the common component that made you feel good about those memories. What was present for you in all three examples? What were you passionate about?

If you think at first that there's nothing consistent about the memories you've listed, think back to the time and place of each situation. Get in touch with what you were feeling then, about the events and about yourself. Avoid narrowing things down; try to stay with broad, generic statements. Perhaps all the items were fun, maybe they all had a partnership component, or perhaps they all made you uneasy at first, but you did them anyway.

The commonality need not be that all the events happened in the same season; what you're looking for is a consistency in how you felt—who you were being, not what was happening externally. Perhaps the accomplishments all went beyond what you thought was possible, or maybe they led to other things that you hadn't even considered. Maybe there was a quality of surprise connected to them, or perhaps they were things you made happen against all odds. The broader the common thread, the better.

GETTING IN TOUCH WITH YOUR LIFE'S PURPOSE

List three specific times in your life, from the day you were born to this moment, when you felt excited and passionate. Look for three special moments about which you can say, "I did that; it felt good." It could be something you did on your own or with others, or something you did for someone else. Perhaps it was having your first child, buying your first house, giving a speech in high school or college, or completing a project at work. Write them down simply and quickly; as you write the first one, the other two will come.

1. _____

_____

_____

2. _____

_____

_____

3. _____

_____

_____

If you wrote down three sports examples, for instance, what exactly was the common thread of passion for you? Were you passionate about playing, winning, competing, or being part of a team? These are very different responses and will take you in very different directions.

Bill Parker, the vice president of the midwest zone of Old Navy, hired me to teach his team to become dream coaches. Bill's dream was that his team would metaphorically go to the Super Bowl and win. This meant they would be champions at their jobs. He had measurable goals for achieving this, including being number one in sales and hiring six hundred new employees that year. In a zone that grew from $400 million to $1 billion in sales in one year, Old Navy is run by people who know how to dream big. Bill's passion for winning inspired his team, and his dream became their dream, as they acquired the skills and resources to achieve their goals and win.

The litmus test is whether or not the consistent element in your memories of passion was something about which you felt excited, but don't be concerned if passion eludes you at first. Some people become passionate about their purpose as soon as they define it. Others may not be sure if the stated purpose is something that truly excites them. You may not experience passion until you're in action on a project; someone else may be turned on by the planning process. If you're having difficulty finding the common thread in all three accomplishments, but you were excited by two of them, you're probably on the right track.

SPEAKING YOUR PURPOSE

By using language that incorporates your newly defined purpose into your speech, you will affirm your passion and move toward having your dream. I call this speaking your purpose, and on page 37 I've listed some examples from people I've worked with. In each case the three memories are listed, followed by the first try at identifying their life's purpose and then their second attempt to speak it in an empowering way. Note that the initial statements of purpose were altered later.

It doesn't matter whether your purpose is single-focused or multidimensional. Imagine using the zoom lens of a camera to capture your life's purpose in the most general way. Then play with the picture until the form, sound, and feel of it is right for you. The writing exercise on page 38 will help you find validating and empowering words to access the passion in your purpose and to remember it always.

Let's say you have a passion for learning and your purpose statement is "to learn constantly." In this case, the next time you are stuck in rush-hour traffic you can say to yourself, "What was my purpose again? Oh, yeah, to learn constantly." Then you can play a language tape or a book on tape and feel good that you are doing something that matters to you.

Here's one more analogy. When you know your purpose and can instantly recall it, it's like walking around with an electrical cord. Look for outlets to plug into, so you can express your passion. Happiness and satisfaction are back in your hands, where they belong.

**Your purpose in life is simply
to help the purpose of the universe.**
—GEORGE BERNARD SHAW

MEMORIES OF PASSION	PURPOSE
1. Becoming a Certified Public Accountant 2. Being promoted to manager 3. Buying a dream house while selling his old home without a broker	To add value to everything I do -or- To make a difference by being different
1. Growing my business 2. Having a special relationship with a great person 3. Rearing two fabulous children	To use my creativity to alter other people's lives -or- To inspire people into action
1. Making it to the U.S. National Racquetball Team 2. Becoming racquetball state champion 3. Striving for a career in racquetball	To have fun while being the best that I can be -or- To go for the gold
1. Having twin daughters 2. Experiences in the wilderness 3. Winning the Small Business Administration's Outstanding Businesswoman Award	To experience the adventure of people and life -or- To live life as an adventure

SPEAKING PASSIONATELY ABOUT YOUR PURPOSE

List all the different ways in which you can complete the following sentence so that, when you think about it and when you speak about it, you feel its underlying passion. Use your three memories of passion to help you.

My life's purpose is:

_____

_____

_____

_____

_____

_____

_____

Rephrase your purpose to speak it in an empowering way and to make it easy to recall:

_____

_____

_____

_____

_____

_____

The Passion Pyramid

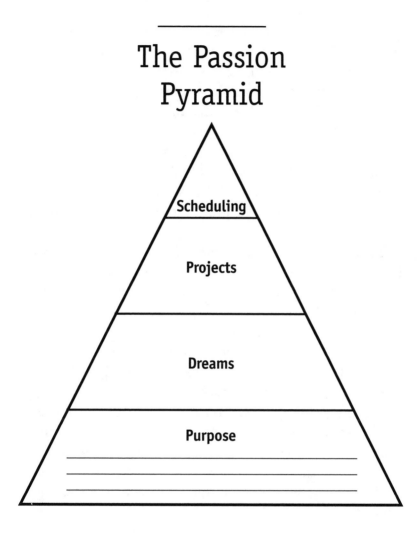

Scheduling

Projects

Dreams

Purpose

The next step is to enter your purpose in the appropriate section at the base of the Passion Pyramid. You will find the Passion Pyramid repeated throughout the book, so you can fill in additional categories as you make choices that will allow your dreams to become reality. You will also find the Passion Scale, appearing for the first time on the next page, duplicated several times in these pages, so that you can rate your passion as we move through each stage. Rate how you feel about your life's purpose. If you are at "interested" or below, ask yourself what's missing from your purpose that would turn you on, and add it. Then rate your passion again.

Here's what I mean. If all three of your memories of passion involved helping others and if your purpose statement is "to help others," but you have little passion for this now, perhaps you are too tired. Adding the word "easily"—"easily to help others"—may prove to be a life-changing action.

To find your passion you looked at the past. Now you also have the opportunity to look ahead. What qualities might lighten up your life and infuse you with more passion? For many, adding an adverb such as "joyously" or "easily" can really make a difference.

If you're wondering how simply adding a word to your purpose statement can change your life, consider this. You are about to create dreams that are an expression of your purpose. From here you will design the plan to have what you want. Start with a solid foundation.

The more passion you have at the beginning of the process, the easier it will be to get what you want. Create a purpose statement that will be a solid foundation to build big dreams upon.

PASSION SCALE

Place an X next to the term that best describes your level of passion about your purpose. Do it right now.

_____ Red hot*
_____ Turned on
_____ Excited
_____ Very interested
_____ Interested
_____ Some possibility
_____ No interest

Real People: KATHLEEN

Kathleen was a successful real estate agent, but her true passion was for new experiences and adventures. She told her colleagues that her dream of all dreams, now that her children were grown, was to live in Italy.

She got a mixed bag of responses, everything from "You go, girl" to "Are you out of your mind?" By the time she came to see me, there was no doubt about her plans: she was moving to Tuscany. With each step she took toward her dream, two things happened. She became more committed and more afraid. By the time she had to put her furniture into storage, she was in need of some real help.

My job was to keep her connected to her passion and her dream. We did this by painting a vivid picture of what her life in

---

*Some people relate to the terms on this Passion Scale and some don't. Perhaps you prefer to use your own terms or to use numbers to rate your passion. Do whatever works for you. Just design a simple measurement so you can continually check in as we move through the process.

Italy would look like. We imagined what kind of house she would live in, what her view would be like, what she would do for a living, and what she would do for fun. I listened for inconsistencies in what she was saying and how she was saying it. We kept facing and removing the obstacles and really freed her to dream big.

I just got my third Christmas card from Kathleen. She is a different person from the woman I met. Year one's card said, "I miss my friends, and although I've been offered many jobs, I am keeping my word to you and following my heart." Year two's card said, "I've met tons of friends and have become very involved in the Florentine community and even started a group to help newcomers. The U.S. Consul General asked me to serve on the board of directors of the Tuscan American Association, to help bring the two cultures together." Year three's card said, "I've yet to discover my true purpose or destiny, but I have learned that timing and patience are everything. I love it here. It has been an incredible life-changing experience, and I would do it all over again. After taking this big step, I feel I could do anything. I am open to whatever opportunities life has to offer me."

Kathleen is alive, joyful, having fun, and living *la dolce vita*. Expressing your passion and following the dreams of your heart is living on purpose.

CHAPTER 4

Dreams: How Do You Want Your Life to Be?

**Go confidently in the direction of your dreams.
Live the life you have imagined.**

—HENRY DAVID THOREAU

NOW THAT YOU'VE DISCOVERED the passion underlying your purpose, the focus will be on the direction in which your life will be moving. You'll need some additional tools on the journey to make your dreams come true; in this chapter you'll learn how to formulate dreams that will steer you on the right course.

Perhaps you're wondering about the difference between your purpose and your dreams. Your purpose is fundamental: it's who you are. Dreams are mechanisms by which to bring your purpose deliberately into day-to-day life. Dreams answer the question, "How do you want your life to be?"

In a business environment we may refer to a dream as a "vision" or a "goal." It doesn't matter what we call our dream. What matters is that we have it. I am delighted to see that many companies are using the word "dream" in everything from marketing campaigns to annual reports. An advertisement for Bank of

America reads, "The size of your savings shouldn't limit the size of your dreams." Another for American Express reads, "Who can help you manage the details of your dream?" The Gap's annual report said, "Where there's a dream, we make it a reality." When I hear this message or when one of these companies hires me to talk about passion and vision in the workplace, I feel this is a business that really cares about its employees and its customers.

Dreams also can help eliminate those aspects of your life that are inconsistent with your purpose. My own purpose, for example, is to joyously self-express; some dreams may make me happy while others may not allow any joy into my life. By measuring my dreams against my purpose, I can tell if what I've chosen will move me forward with passion to live the life I want, or is it more about a "should," a duty or a self-imposed responsibility. If, like me, you tend to be overly goal-oriented, this activity is not meant to turn obligations into dreams. Yes, you have to pay the rent and handle other responsibilities, but those activities get scheduled into reality anyway. Creating dreams is about getting your life where you want it to be. For instance, if you have a specific financial issue, create a dream within the economic area that expresses who you are. The financial dream for a person who wants to live life as an adventure may be different from the financial dream for someone who wants to be in a committed family relationship.

Developing dreams is part of the process for gaining insight into what matters or doesn't matter to you. Here we're trying to eliminate inconsistencies; these dreams are to be fulfilled in support of your life's purpose. This is different from the traditional goal-setting process in business, where a desired outcome is selected and a completion date is designated. The funny thing about the goal-setting process is that when you set a date to do something, either you accomplish it or you move the date.

Dreams answer the question

"How do you want your life to be?"

To achieve your dream, you need to do everything from this point forward from the perspective of your purpose. Keep checking in, making sure you're passionate about your dreams. Go for alignment as we move up the Passion Pyramid.

I call this living on purpose. It's essential to *be* the purpose you defined at the foundation of the Passion Pyramid. Even though you may not feel at ease yet with your stated purpose, assume that you will; the comfort from living life on purpose will follow. Just trust. Living on purpose is the most joyful and fulfilling way I know to live.

It's too early in the process to expect that everything in your life will automatically align with your purpose. In fact, while you're learning, it makes more sense to focus on a particular facet of your life. To help you choose which aspects you want to concentrate on, use the Dream Areas exercise on page 49. Decide not only which areas you want to pinpoint but also what there is about them that needs attention.

Perhaps your relationships are boring and you want to establish relationships that are fun, or you wish to find your dream mate. Maybe you want to become involved in your community in a more creative, innovative, or substantive way than before. Use the Dream Areas form to list the facets of your life and what there is to explore about them; there is an exercise later in this chapter to guide you through the actual exploration. When you complete the Dream Areas form, review it and choose one category to use as you go through this book. When you've mastered one area by following it through to the book's conclusion, you can go back and use the same techniques to make your dreams come true in the other areas of your life. This process is tried and true on all types of dreams. And if you choose to work on multiple dreams simultaneously, just be sure to follow all the steps for each one completely.

Remember that your dreams are both the way to incorporate your purpose into daily life and a tool for eliminating inconsistencies. Be sure that there is no disparity between the dreams listed on the Dream Areas form and your life's purpose. One way to do this is to role-play—to "be" your life's purpose—and to ask, "If this is who I am as my life's purpose, is this an appropriate dream? Does it line up? Does it turn me on?"

Don't carry any dreams over from an old list or from what your parents wanted; the values you develop now are the ones by which you will live your future life. Maybe you will develop dreams that seem contradictory. If so, don't worry that you can't figure out right now how you're going to have it all. Suppose, for example, that you want both a stable home life and exciting world travel. Another way to say this is that you want to love your work and still have time to love and be there for your family. You want it all.

My brother, who works for 3Com, just got back from the company's European Users Conference in Monte Carlo. He took his wife, as did the other managers. They wined and dined their customers and had a wonderful time making new friends. Monaco is filled with adventure and romance. Rekindling a little passion in his marriage certainly won't hurt his performance at work. While

Perhaps you hear a small voice saying
that you can't have what you want,
that you don't have the time or the resources
to take on anything else. Don't worry
about that nagging voice;
you don't have to do anything yet.
Neither do you have to base
new dreams on the past.

Right now you simply have to
be who you say you are;
you can create a whole new life
from this moment forward.
Ask yourself what dreams
a person with your life's purpose would want.
Then listen for the answers.

there, he cut his playtime short one day to go back to his room for a massage and a conference call. I'm just wondering if he did them both at the same time.

Believe it's possible to take your home life on the road, or believe you can have fun at work and that you'll discover a whole new set of possible ways to have it all. Play with this idea.

You aren't looking for inconsistencies among your dreams, but for dreams that are incompatible with your purpose. When you respond to the question, "Is this dream appropriate to my purpose?" you want to feel excited about the answer. Use the Passion Scale to check in and see how you feel about each dream area.

Eventually you will want ease to appear in every facet of your life. For the moment focus on the area you chose to explore throughout this book. The Garden of Possibility exercise on page 51 will help you appraise your dreams and align them with your purpose.

Let's walk through the Garden of Possibility process using the details that I used to focus on the professional area of my life. I picked this area because redefining my career really mattered to me at the time I did this exercise. You'll want to choose whatever area is pressing or of interest to you right now.

When I entered the garden, I felt completely at ease because it was landscaped with my purpose—to joyously self-express. Seeded with hope, the garden allowed me to explore my professional dream: to have a new career that expresses who I am in the world. Filled with the passion coming from my purpose, I created the professional dream to have work that would be a joyous expression of who I am. That means having work that is play, that is lucrative, and that allows plenty of time for family and friends. Sound like a fantasy? Well, it's not. Now that I know I want all of it, I can design a plan for getting it.

Should the voice of doubt begin to nag you here, don't fret.

We will address your doubts and concerns in the beliefs section. For now I want you to really begin to dream, to imagine how you want your life to be, without worrying about whether you can actually have it or not. That's why I call it dreaming!

DREAM AREAS TO EXPLORE

The categories listed below are aspects of life you might want to explore initially. You don't have to limit yourself to these; select areas that are important to you.

If my life's purpose is _____

_____

My community dream is _____

_____

My family dream is _____

_____

My financial dream is _____

_____

My fitness dream is _____

_____

My friendship dream is _____

_____

My fun dream is _____

_____

My health and well-being dream is _____

_____

My outrageous dream is _____

_____

My personal dream is _____

_____

My professional dream is _____

_____

My recreational dream is _____

_____

My relationships dream is _____

_____

My other dreams are _____

_____

_____

_____

_____

_____

_____

_____

PASSION SCALE

Place an X next to the term that best describes your level of passion about your dreams. Do it right now.

_____ Red hot
_____ Turned on
_____ Excited
_____ Very interested
_____ Interested
_____ Some possibility
_____ No interest

THE GARDEN OF POSSIBILITY

This exercise will help you create dreams that are consistent with your life's purpose. You may want to read this page aloud into a tape recorder, then play it back. The key to the garden of possibility is passion. The passion lives inside your heart and is always present when you're living on purpose. Begin by closing your eyes and taking several deep breaths. Relax.

With your eyes closed, envision a beautiful garden. It's lovely and inviting, and it's filled with your favorite flowers and trees. You easily make your way into the garden, and you feel at home in this lovely place that holds your purpose.

Find a comfortable spot to sit or lie down, perhaps near a shady tree or next to an fragrant flower bed. Relax; you feel completely at home living on purpose.

It's a beautiful day; the sky is clear blue with puffy white clouds, and the air is just the right temperature. You're completely relaxed and at ease in your purpose, filled with passion, knowing there's unlimited possibility everywhere.

You reinforce your sense of purpose by finishing this sentence: "My life's purpose is . . ." You feel grounded in your purpose, and from that perspective you begin to look at how you want life to be.

With your eyes closed, look at the area of your life you chose to explore. If you are focusing on the professional area, complete this sentence: "My professional dream is to . . ." Perhaps you'd like to open your eyes and write it down; if you prefer to keep your eyes closed, fill it in later.

After you've finished exploring the area you selected, relax in perfect comfort in the garden. Notice if any images or feelings come up, and feel free to write them down as well. Take a last look around, and experience the power that envelops you. Feel the clarity of your life's purpose, and know that your dream in the area you examined is in perfect alignment with your purpose and that anything is possible.

By the time you complete this exercise you will have identified at least one dream in your chosen area. You can have more than one if you wish, but it's less important to designate many dreams than it is to be clear that the dreams express your life's purpose.

When you're ready to leave the Garden of Possibilities, breathe deeply. Relax. Open your eyes when you are ready. You will have a clear memory of everything that happened during the exercise.

On the Passion Pyramid write "My life's purpose is . . ." In the area you chose, complete this sentence: "My dream is to . . ."

_____

_____

In my garden exercise, I focused on my professional life, but that's not the only area for which I have developed dreams. In the personal area, my dream is to develop partnerships with individuals who are creative visionaries so we can produce results that have a positive impact on others. In the area of well-being, I dream of being healthier and more physically fit at forty-five than I was at thirty-five. In the area of relationships, I hope to be in a loving partnership with my life's companion. In the area of friendship, I dream of having friends worldwide. In the financial area, I want to shop without looking at price tags. Notice that each dream is an expression of my purpose.

Don't be stingy when you develop dreams; put into them everything that you want. When I noted that one of my dreams was to have friends worldwide, I didn't say merely that I wanted friends. I am committed to having friends everywhere on the planet, which suggests travel as another dream. If you don't develop your objectives in a way that expresses your life's purpose, your ability to make your dreams come true will be short-circuited.

The power that you experience all around you comes from having passion within you. However, you don't have to do this exercise to feel the excitement.

In the blank space on page 55, commit yourself to focusing on a specific area of your life by filling in the blank. Then on page 54 write your purpose once again in the foundation of the Passion Pyramid, and this time, include the dream you'll be working on. For example, my own life's purpose is to joyously self-express, and my dream in the professional area is to have work that expresses who I am in the world. There is alignment as I move from my purpose to my dreams.

The Passion Pyramid

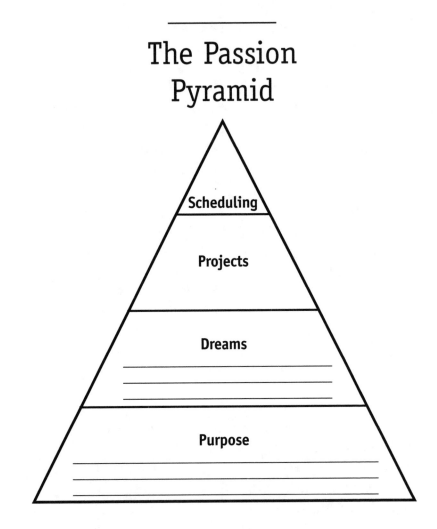

When you fill in the base of the pyramid, commit your purpose to paper fully and with passion, and state the dream by which you will live your life on purpose.

Fill in the blank by stating the aspect of your life on which you intend to concentrate. I am committed to focusing on a specific area of my life at this time. The area I'm going to focus on is:

_____

_____

Real People: BETH AND STEPHEN

Since Beth's parents had always worked together, her dream was that she would have a business partner, too. She didn't realize it would be her future husband. Beth and Stephen met and married because they loved each other's laugh, among other things. They have a passion for fun. Beth had asked all her previous boyfriends if they would ever leave New York with her and move to San Francisco, which was part of her dream. When she met Stephen and he said yes, she knew he was a keeper.

They had been married for a year and living in a small Manhattan apartment when Stephen came home from his job at the Learning Annex and mentioned that the company was selling its San Francisco location. The Learning Annex, America's leading alternative adult education organization, offers courses on everything from sushi making to singing, and presents lectures by some of the best-selling authors and most highly acclaimed speakers of our time. Beth said, "Why don't we buy it and move out there?" To her total shock, he said, "Okay," and within four months, during one of the biggest blizzards in New York, they packed up and moved west to pursue their dream.

They borrowed money from their family and tapped out their credit cards. They had a slow start because the Gulf War began on the day they opened their doors. Everyone was home watching CNN, and no one was attending classes. With Beth's expertise in writing, public relations, and graphic design, she got the word out. Their efforts paid off. Within one year they took over locations in Los Angeles, San Diego, and eventually, even New York. They are now thriving and are listed as one of the top 100 companies in San Francisco.

Beth and Stephen know how to dream. They believed in their dream and demonstrated it. Here are some of Beth's other dreams. Keep her purpose in mind: to have fun and enjoy life. Her personal dream is to express herself creatively and to empower others to be great. Her professional dream is that their company will be known worldwide for enhancing the quality of people's lives through powerful, inspirational, nurturing, and insightful seminars. Her relationship dream is to have a loving family and be a great mom. Her health dream is to be strong and flexible, physically and emotionally. Her financial dream is to own a beautiful home in a peaceful setting, and her fun dream is to laugh a lot.

As you achieve your dreams, you build confidence and can dream bigger. After years of trying to get pregnant, Beth and Stephen began to explore the adoption process. They heard many horror stories, but they had learned how to face and surmount obstacles. Beth found a potential birth mother on the Internet and when they all met, they loved each other. This mom-to-be had a great sense of humor and felt right to Beth. She was a young single woman and did not want to keep her baby.

The young woman lived in Missouri where the adoption laws were very prohibitive, so Beth and Stephen moved her to be near them. Beth found her a nice apartment, paid all of her living expenses and doctor bills, and even hired a birth coach. Beth and Stephen were with the birth mother a lot during those last few months, and they were present at the birth of their beautiful new daughter. Stephen even cut the cord. And Casey Bea, the newest edition to this DreamTeam, laughs all the time. She is a daily reminder that anything is possible when you believe in your dreams.

When you're standing in your life's purpose,

the passion is always there,

and possibilities live everywhere.

You feel powerful, and capable

of making your dreams come true.

CHAPTER 5

A Dream
That Inspires You

**All our dreams can come true
if we have the courage to pursue them.**

—WALT DISNEY

A DEAR FRIEND ONCE TOLD ME that turning a dream into a project is a way to project yourself into the future. In this chapter, you will learn how to define your dream, how to develop it, and how to initiate it in the form of a project.

Clarifying the dream is the critical step that most people omit, largely because they don't perceive their dream as something real, specific, and attainable. If your dream arises from your purpose, you can create a project to make your dream a reality.

The power to develop a viable project depends, first, on your ability to define your dream in a way that inspires you. The project, which will have specific and measurable results, makes the dream attainable. Moreover, ease will occur as new possibilities open up during the definition phase, and you can start to launch yourself into a different dimension of living life.

Sometimes acting on a dream is as simple as choosing a date by which it will happen. Other times, the plan is not as simple as it sounds—having a general idea of how you want your dream to be may not be enough to know exactly how to achieve it.

Clarifying your dream

is crucial to your success.

DESCRIBING YOUR DREAM TO A TEE

When a dream first enters your consciousness, you may not be able to see with clarity what it looks like. Often a dream starts in the subconscious and remains a nebulous idea floating around in the back of your mind. In order for your dream to come true, you must get it out of your head.

Speaking of floating, one year at Dream University®, Marieta, who had been in the army for ten years and who now worked at the post office, found herself relaxing in the hot tub. Hanging out with new friends, every time she spoke, she made people laugh. She was quick and witty. Other people's laughter helped Marieta discover her passion for being funny. That evening she came to our workshop and did five minutes of stand-up comedy about stamps and life at the post office, original material that she had just created. Our howling at her jokes gave her the confidence to attend a weekly comedy class, and at forty-five years of age she did her first showcase at the Punch Line Comedy Club. When *More* magazine called me looking for stories about people taking risks at midlife, I gave them Marieta's name, and she wound up as the subject of a full-page story that called her the Joker.

There are many different ways to gain access to the details of your dream. Some people like to do it through writing exercises; some carry on conversations with others about their dream; and some prefer talking into a tape recorder. One client told me she actually thinks by talking.

Recently I was hired as a spokesperson for a dream contest. I traveled around the country appearing on television and inviting people to write a short essay, poem, or story about how they would spend money if they won it for the sole purpose of realizing a dream. In this contest, called Taste How Good Life Can Be and sponsored by Sunsweet Prunes, we gave away three prizes of $50,000 each. Sunsweet's criterion was based on creativity, and I was surprised at how many entries played it safe and were realistic rather than going for their heart's desire.

I hope you will use this opportunity to really dream. In the Details of My Dream, page 62, I have provided room for you to write out all the aspects of your dream. This exercise is a powerful way to get the dream out of your head and allow it to become real. Use the exercise to get in touch with all the resources that can help to develop your dream; use it also to get a clear image of what you want, to get the level of detail behind the initial statement of your dream. Notice whether you believe it's possible to have your dream, but don't let your beliefs limit you. We'll deal with them shortly.

If you aren't happy with what you write down at first, you aren't bound to it. Rewrite it more than once, if necessary. As you start to gain clarity, what gets committed to paper will begin to feel right. At the end of this chapter are some Real People stories that illustrate how these techniques work for people who have passion about their purpose and who have defined their dreams accordingly.

SEEKING INSPIRATION

The specifics of your dream may not all come at one sitting; perhaps it will take a few days, even a few weeks. If you need inspiration to complete the exercise, go to the library, go to plays or movies, or rent children's videos like *Beauty and the Beast* and *Mary Poppins*. You might want to travel. Keep your eyes, mind, and heart open.

The dreams you have while sleeping are another great place to find out about your waking dream. No doubt you've heard this suggestion before, but it's worth repeating: place a pad or a cassette recorder next to your bed. Tell yourself before you fall asleep to remember your nocturnal dreams, and eventually you will. In fact, you can plant a question in your subconscious before going to sleep—for example, "I want more information about this decision I have to make"—and see what comes up during the night.

You can also daydream by relaxing and letting your mind wander. Be alert to what excites you. Perhaps you admire someone's beautiful office, somebody's lovely home, parts of a job someone is performing. When you are building your dream and imagining its details, feel free to include in your dream what you like about other people's reality. This is one place where borrowing really pays off.

Perhaps you're a woman who wants a beautiful dress from a particular designer. Maybe your dream can start with something small, like an accessory or a great pair of new shoes. Make an investment in yourself and bring part of your dream into reality; you will be that much closer to having it all. If you dream of traveling around the world, but you don't have the time or the money right now, start where you can. Take a day trip, go on a hike, go to a nearby lake, stream, or ocean. Don't deprive yourself of something just because you can't have it all. Every step you take toward your dream puts you closer to your desired result.

DETAILS OF MY DREAM

Complete the following sentences with as many details of your dream as you can summon. You can write your description in sentences, you can make a skeleton outline, or you can draw pictures.

Play with this exercise; use your imagination; try different alternatives. Write down something that you want in your dream, and if it doesn't feel right, change it. You are the author of your own dream. I hope you need more space than this to describe it.

My dream, or the essence of my dream, is _____

_____

_____

The details of my dream include _____

_____

_____

_____

_____

_____

_____

_____

_____

_____

_____

If you can bring something simple

into your life right now

that will make you feel good,

do so and begin to live your dream immediately.

Some people can bring their dream into focus by using photographs. Perhaps you want to live near the ocean and have a view of the mountains. Find a picture of what you want, put it into your reality by posting it on the bathroom mirror, and start connecting to it. If you begin to think about it as existing now, it will become real.

Whatever you do to stimulate your mind, pay attention and notice what feels good. Relax and have fun. You are creating a design for your life, letting your dream come forward and elaborating on it. Remember, this is your dream; you don't have to choose what you don't want, what you think you should have, what you've always had, or what your mother wanted you to have.

Start by thinking about your dream as real. Visualize it, and then expand your visualization. Learn to speak about it clearly; the more you speak about it, the more detailed it will become. Write, plan, and brainstorm about it. Get into action, any kind of action. It's your dream; start living it now.

Now rate yourself on the Passion Scale. Place an X next to the term that best describes your level of passion about your dream. Do it right now.

PASSION SCALE

_____ Red hot
_____ Turned on
_____ Excited
_____ Very interested
_____ Interested
_____ Some possibility
_____ No interest

Real People: GEORGE

George's purpose—to live life as an adventure—was embodied by his general desire to bring adventure into every facet of his life. However, George was having trouble finding a way to realize his dream, which was to take a lengthy, luxurious fishing trip to a tropical location. When George first started to speak about his dream, he gave many reasons why he couldn't have it. The more he spoke about the dream, the more committed he became. Once he learned to stand in his purpose, the dream stopped being a fuzzy thing in the back of his mind and started to take on structure. He began to paint a word picture of his dream.

George asked himself questions and gave himself answers, putting into writing exactly what his dream would look like. The first question George asked was how long he wanted the dream trip to be. He was surprised to discover that he wanted it to last at least a month. Who else was with him? He was alone. Where was he living? In a tropical paradise.

As he wrote, George came up with more and more questions, and as he answered them he became clearer and clearer about his dream. He put into his dream everything he wanted and left out everything he didn't want. He decided, for instance, to forsake his alarm clock and sleep until he awakened naturally. Even in his tropical paradise, however, he wanted the *Wall Street Journal* delivered daily, because he didn't want to be completely out of touch with the world. He didn't want to do any cooking, so he saw himself jogging on the beach and returning to a delicious breakfast prepared by a chef.

Picture yourself
already living your dream.

Then George started to ask more about how he would spend his days. He visualized owning a small boat; he saw himself using the boat to take fishing trips, both for fun and for the opportunity to meet other people. He continued designing into his dream all that he wanted. George also expressed some concern about being away for an extended period of time. He wondered what impact his trip would have on the people and the business he was leaving behind. He tempered his anxiety by answering these questions positively: he decided, and his family verified, that they would function well in his absence and that his business would continue to thrive.

Once he was clear about his dream, George resolved to try it out on a short-term basis. He determined that, within three months, he would take a two-week fishing trip to an exotic place. He chose Costa Rica, he scheduled the trip, and he went.

George had a wonderful time, and he learned a few important things. The first lesson was that two weeks was long enough. The fishing was great and so was the adventure, but he missed his family, and after two weeks he'd had enough of doing the same thing every day.

He also observed that bringing adventure into his life deepened his relationship with his family. There's renewed romance in his marriage, and now he's able to bring adventure into his life anytime he chooses to do so. Like George, you will discover that one magical adventure can lead to many more, if you stop holding back and go for what you want.

Real People: LYNN

Lynn had been a vice president of marketing for many years. She was burned out and knew exactly what she wanted. Her dream was to have fifty-two vacation days a year without a reduction in her salary.

She proposed this to the company president, who at first had a hard time accepting it. But she was skilled at painting a picture and showed him the benefits. She pointed out that she could get the company operating at maximum efficiency and that she would train her staff to function well even when she wasn't there on a day-to-day basis.

When Lynn took a little more time, she got crystal clear about her true dream. What she really wanted was to travel. That was what she was passionate about. But to travel she needed freedom and flexibility. Getting an extra day off here and there or working a four-day week was not what she needed.

Lynn described her dream to her boss and started to prepare her subordinates for the transition. When the negotiations were done, she got what she wanted: she went part-time, working 80 percent of the time, without any cut in pay.

Even after she achieved her dream, however, she kept the door open, and another wonderful opportunity surfaced when she realized that she had left something on the table. Her company bartered with an airline, trading baked goods for airline tickets. If she could get some of those tickets, that would be a dream come true. She went back in and told her boss that one more thing would make her really happy. The boss agreed she could have eight free round-trip tickets to help fulfill her dream of world travel.

Ask for what you want.

Real People: BRIAN

Brian's purpose was to make a contribution to society. His professional dream was to use his skills and expertise in a career that he loved. His project was to start a new business and to own his own company. The problem was that Brian didn't know what his new company would do. He had a general sense of what he wanted, but he was stymied about the particulars.

Following his passion, Brian decided to create a problem-solving organization for designing and implementing social projects for children and their families. Then he set a specific date, deciding to be open for business by the first of the new year.

Still, Brian didn't know what his dream looked like. As he fleshed out the details, he saw that he could train people to become community leaders. He envisioned creating a variety of products that would further his mission—a children's radio show, a newsletter, periodicals about literacy, a videotape training series.

Now that Brian could "see" his new company's form, he had to decide where it would be located, how his office would be decorated, what the logo would look like, who would work for the company, how they would be perceived in the community, and where he would get funding. The clarity of his dream kept him inspired and in action. As he moved forward, his next steps became more obvious and, in turn, he became more motivated than ever. There was no stopping him now, as we'll see later.

Discovery consists of seeing

what everybody has seen and

thinking what nobody has thought.

—ALBERT SZENT-GYÖRGI VON NAGYRAPOLT

Real People: LARRY

Larry, whose purpose was to create powerful partnerships and intimate relationships, had as his dream to become a partner with anyone at any time he chose. At first Larry's dream was to double his business—a big dream without any definition. Envisioning the details of what his dream would look like, Larry imagined that his company would have earnings of $3 million by the end of the year and $10 million within five years. Keep in mind that he simply made this up and stated it as his dream. This was an essential step.

The more you speak and write

about your dream,

the sooner you'll live it.

The more Larry wrote about his dream, the more specific he became. He wanted everyone in his company to work in partnership. He wanted to be well known and respected as a leader in his field. He wanted the people with whom he worked to have the best credentials and to offer top-quality service.

Larry chose a date by which he wanted to have at least three domestic offices, although eventually he wanted branches worldwide. He wanted to own his office building and have his name on the outside of it. He wanted a personal assistant, a right-hand person who would take good care of him. His dream was that this person would make his job and his life easier while fulfilling his or her own dreams.

Finally, Larry understood that it was possible to determine how the whole dream would look, not just the financial aspect, which had been his first concern. By gaining clarity about the entire dream, Larry was able to create projects that would help him easily achieve it.

The bridge to make

all dreams come true

is made up of our thoughts and our words.

Your dream starts here.

CHAPTER 6

Where You Are and Where You Want to Be

**We can chart our future clearly and wisely
only when we know the path which led to the present.**

—ADLAI E. STEVENSON

YOU HAVE BEGUN TO GAIN some clarity about where you want to be in life, but the road to your dreams starts where you are now. You can't travel that road successfully if you don't know where you are now or if you're standing in quicksand.

An honest assessment of your current situation may lead to the disappointing discovery that you're not even close to where you intend to go. Sorry, I know reality can sometimes sting, but recognizing it is an essential part of the dream formula. Your challenge is to use your existing position, no matter how far it is from your dream, to create the momentum to propel you forward.

I can't stress enough the importance of making an honest assessment of where you are now. Starting with inaccurate information will lead to unwise decisions about what you have to do and how far you have to go to reach your dream. You cannot build your new life on a strong base if you deny any part of your present existence. Get everything out on the table; list where you are with respect to each of the facets. Be brutally honest, but don't become discouraged; all of us face a number of impediments to having the life we want.

Where you are now

is simply where you are now.

There is no value judgment attached to it.

No doubt you will find that you're at a different place in each aspect of your life—closer to your dream in some and farther away from it in others. That's a typical pattern. Ask yourself where you are not only with respect to your dream but also with regard to your support system, your financial situation, and your feelings. What are your concerns and beliefs? We'll take a closer look at attitudes in the next chapter; right now it's important merely to recognize that you have opinions about where you are compared with where you want to be.

If you need a clue about where to start evaluating, take another look at the completed Dream Areas form in Chapter 4. For example, where are you currently with respect to the personal, professional, health, and family aspects of your life? What concerns do you have in these areas? Do you worry that going for your dream will take up too much time? Perhaps you don't believe it's possible to make your dream come true. For now just notice what you are thinking and what you are feeling. We will work with all of it, one step at a time, as we progress through this together.

TENSION CAN BE USEFUL

The difference between where you are and where you want to be can create tension. Am I right? The challenge is to learn to use this tension as a creative force. Can you be more committed to where you want to be? Picture the tension in a slingshot as you pull on it, and the release of tension as you relax the pull. Tension will resolve itself naturally in whatever direction there is more focus. Therefore, all things being equal, something will move in whichever direction it is aimed.

The difference between where you are

and where you want to be

will create healthy tension

that can move you forward.

Thus, if you put "where you want to be" (your dream) within the slingshot in place of "where you are" (your reality), the difference between where you are and where you want to be will create tension; the direction in which you aim the slingshot is the way the slingshot is going to shoot.

The bottom line is this: On a day-to-day basis, are you more committed to your dream or to your reality? The evidence will be clear in the action you are taking or not taking. Just watch what you are doing and not doing. It will be very telling.

If you know with clarity where you want to go, you can focus your attention on your dream and use the information about where you are to propel you forward. If you find that you're far removed from your goal, don't despair; the tension in the distance from where you are to where you want to be may launch you even faster in whatever direction you choose.

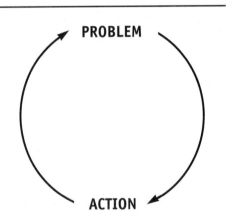

PROBLEM

ACTION

Taking action just to eliminate or minimize the problem will eventually lead you back to the problem.

You can't be thrust forward, however, unless you stay clear and honest about your current position. When you start to negotiate with yourself—"Oh, this isn't so bad; I've been here for a couple of years, so a little while longer won't hurt"—you dilute or eliminate the dynamic. It's the tension that moves you forward.

PROBLEM-SOLVING

There's a different kind of energy involved when moving toward what you want than there is when moving away from what you don't want. For instance, you may have a problem with debt. If you take action to eradicate the debt, you're likely to stop taking action as the problem starts to go away. Your inaction can then lead right back to the problem.

Consider the example of countries whose people are starving. In the past, the action we've taken is to feed those who are hungry. As soon as people are no longer starving, the birthrate increases, the population becomes restless, and the problem gets worse. In other words, when some progress has been made, people don't try as hard; they feel they can let up a bit in light of what they've already done, and soon they're back to where they started. Managing the problem always leads back to the problem. One solution is to feed those who are hungry while simultaneously teaching them how to produce food for themselves.

To avoid simply managing the problem, set up your life so that you're always moving toward what you want. Perhaps your dream is to be healthy and physically fit, but you are overweight. If your dream is to be healthy and vibrant, to feel and look good, a different kind of energy will be applied than to the drudgery of getting rid of the weight by diet and exercise. In the latter scenario, the food intake tends to increase and the exercise tends to stop as soon as the weight begins to drop. When my scale showed I had dropped a few pounds, I would go looking for brownies, until I realized this was a vicious and energy-draining cycle. It's this simple. If my dream is to be physically fit and my reality is that I am overweight, I can tell which one I am more committed to by what I am putting in my mouth. Once I saw this, I began practicing new and healthier habits.

The critical question now centers on whether you're more committed to remaining where you are or to getting where you want to be. The difference between the two is what will propel you forward. Below is an exercise you can use to write a list of where you are and where you want to be.

POSITIONING YOURSELF

List where you are in each of the areas of your life compared to where you want to be with respect to your dream. Be brutally honest; you can't know where you want to go until you know with certainty where you are now. Don't judge; just write it all down.

CATEGORY	WHERE I AM NOW	WHERE I WANT TO BE
Personal	_____	_____
	_____	_____
Professional	_____	_____
	_____	_____
Family	_____	_____
	_____	_____

Friends

_____   _____

_____   _____

Health and
Well-Being

_____   _____

Financial

_____   _____

_____   _____

Fun

_____   _____

_____   _____

Recreation

_____   _____

_____   _____

Relationships

_____   _____

_____   _____

Fitness

_____   _____

_____   _____

Community

_____   _____

_____   _____

Outrageous, Other   _____   _____

As you look at where you are, you are likely to hear an inner
voice whispering all your limitations—all your attitudes and
beliefs, concerns, fears, worries, and tales about why you can't
have what you want. Fortunately, your positive attitudes and
beliefs also will arise—that is, you do believe your dream is pos-

sible, it's something you've always wanted, something to which you're committed, something you know you can have.

People frequently sabotage themselves by putting their attitudes, beliefs, and fears into their dream. If you're putting your concerns into your dreams, your fears will become bigger and seem more real as you move closer to getting what you want. Your concerns don't belong in your dream; they're part of where you are now, not where you're going. If your dream is to be successful, keep in the "Where I Am Now" section the fear that you won't have time for friends and family. Assume for the "Where I Want to Be" section that, in achieving the dream, you will have all the time you desire to enjoy your success, your friends, and your family.

Creating a record of where you are compared to where you want to be is an effective exercise. Whether you're writing it out or speaking it into a tape recorder, you will have it available to use as positive reinforcement.

Are you more committed

to remaining where you are

or to getting where you want to be?

Reread the exercise or play back your recording of it whenever you want to ensure that where you want to be is clearly defined and devoid of your fears about getting there.

Real People: TATIANA

My position as president of the National Association of Women Business Owners in Washington, D.C., afforded me some wonderful opportunities. One of my favorites was the pleasure of meeting with women from all over the world. One afternoon I met Tatiana for tea. She was visiting from Russia.

"I envy you," she began, "because you are a woman business owner."

I was confused, "Tatiana, I don't get it. You're a woman, too, and you have a business."

"I don't charge for my services." She explained that she represented several up-and-coming artists, but she didn't believe her artists could afford to pay her. I had an idea.

"Tatiana, I am exploring doing business with your country. Can I ask you some questions?" She was eager to comply.

After about ten minutes, I thanked her and told her that I believe in paying for information. At first she refused, but when she saw I was only talking about one dollar, she laughed and took it.

I said, "You have just been paid for a service you provided. You are now a woman business owner."

A year went by before I saw her again. She strode in to my office and announced that now she was indeed a woman business owner.

"I went home and started to charge for my service," she said. "The amazing thing was they were willing to pay me a service fee up front before I even closed a deal for them. I represent some of the finest artists in my country, and one is a goldsmith."

She showed me a beautiful gold box that she was wearing on a chain around her neck. I could see there was something it. It was the dollar bill that I had given her.

"You believed in me before I did," she said. "Once you helped me see what was possible, I knew it was what I wanted."

Real People: MARILEE

I met Marilee at a cocktail party. She was eager to talk about her dream of moving from being a first grade teacher to becoming known worldwide as a great clothing designer. I became exhausted as she mapped out for me what sounded like the longest, hardest road imaginable.

"Do you really think it needs to be that hard?" I asked. She was intrigued and asked, "How would you do it?"

"Do you have talent? Are you good?"

"I am very good," she confidently replied.

"Then bank on your talent. Prove by taking action that you are more committed to your dream than you are to your reality or your doubt."

A few weeks later a package arrived at my home from Marilee with magnificent sketches of outfits. One was a hot pink skirt-and-pants suit, another was a sexy little purple dress, and a third was a red evening gown, with a note that said, "I picture you wearing this for dinner at the White House." Although I have yet to be invited, I was relieved to know that I would have something to wear. And I loved that she was dreaming for me. I called her and said, "Make the outfits." Which she did.

Besides being on her DreamTeam by purchasing the outfits, I told some friends about her, and then the word was out. Marilee told me that I gave her the greatest gift when I said, "These are fabulous. I believe in your dream." With that vote of confidence, she enrolled in the Fashion Institute of Design Merchandising, and in less than three years and with an investment of $17,000, she graduated with a 4.0 average.

Marilee has been invited to design women's golf wear and band uniforms. At the Los Angeles County Museum of Art, someone wanted to buy the jacket off her back and produce a line of them. At this point she must reassess, because where she is is very different from where she was three years ago, and where she wants to be is also different.

She sat down and wrote a compelling letter to Liz Claiborne, her dream company, describing her vision of being a top executive designer for them. But then fear and doubt kicked in. As a single mom of a young son who has diabetes, she has real concerns. As a teacher, which she still is, she has a pension and a good salary. The idea of becoming as associate designer and initially cutting her salary in half was terrifying. To date, she has yet to mail the letter to Liz Claiborne. She's afraid they'll hire her, and then what?

Marilee is at a critical juncture. Her commitment to her dream was enough to get her to where she is now. The next step is for her to work on her limiting beliefs and to get them out of her dream before she completely sabotages it. She found a mentor (more about this in Chapter 12) who told her that her dream job will come if she stays committed to it, believes in it, and takes action, one step at a time every day, to keep the dream moving forward. I couldn't have said it better myself.

CHAPTER 7

Breaking Through Barriers and Beliefs

Your beliefs are never neutral. They either move you forward or hold you back. And you choose what you will believe.

—MARCIA WIEDER

ALL OF US HAVE ATTITUDES and beliefs about the various aspects of our lives. Your opinions are long-term parts of who you are: if you're thirty years old they've been developing for thirty years; if you're forty they've been evolving for forty years. Attitudes and beliefs are not always negative and not always barriers to achieving what you want; even if they are, fear not, it's possible to use them to your advantage.

The decisions and choices you make ultimately result from the attitudes and beliefs you hold about everything in your life. The process looks like this:

Your attitudes and beliefs
<create>
your thoughts and feelings
<which determine>
your choices and decisions

Attitudes and beliefs are at the core of how you react in the world. No matter how or why you developed them, it's crucial that you take responsibility for them and evaluate them honestly. The naked truth about your attitudes and beliefs in this chapter is as important as your honest assessment in the last chapter of where you are versus where you want to be.

In my workshops I often ask, "How many people believe they can make their dreams come true?" A few hands go up. Then I ask, "How many believe it's *possible* to make your dreams come true?" Most hands go up.

"So what will it take to move you from possible to probable?" I ask.

Then I inquire, "Who's living in the home of your dreams, driving the car of your dreams, enjoying the relationship or job of your dreams?" Sadly, few respond favorably.

If you believe it's possible to make your dreams come true and yet you don't do it, there's a gap between where you are and where you want to be. This gap is composed of your attitudes and beliefs. The bigger the negative beliefs, the wider the gap.

Some attitudes and beliefs are positive and supportive of the overall dream, and you can use them to get what you want. However, your negative attitudes and beliefs may become obstacles to achieving your dream. For example, you may believe that you can't have what you want, that you can get only a portion of it, or that getting what you want will create more problems so it's better not to try. You might think that you're facing barriers you can't move beyond: your sex, your height, your lack of education, your work experience.

Attitudes and beliefs are never neutral. They either move you forward or hold you back. The most important point I can make here is this: We choose what we believe. Whether you choose a negative or a positive belief, it's much more effective to deal with it now than later.

MY BELIEFS

Create a list about where you are and where you want to be:

CATEGORY	MY BELIEFS ABOUT WHERE I AM NOW	MY BELIEFS ABOUT WHERE I WANT TO BE
_____	_____	_____
_____	_____	_____
_____	_____	_____
_____	_____	_____
_____	_____	_____
_____	_____	_____
_____	_____	_____
_____	_____	_____
_____	_____	_____
_____	_____	_____
_____	_____	_____
_____	_____	_____

Positive beliefs are your allies; they're on your side as you design the life you want. Those that are negative can sabotage you, especially if they get inserted into your dream or if they're perceived as the biggest part of where you are now. By far the number one way we sabotage our dreams is by projecting our fears, doubts, and concerns into our dreams. By becoming aware of this major sabotaging pattern, you can change your life for the better.

Unexamined negative attitudes can become bigger than your dream and turn into insurmountable obstacles after you're already on the road to what you want. If that happens, and you're stopped en route, you're unlikely to reach your dream.

Alternatively, negative attitudes and beliefs don't have to be as menacing as they may seem at first. Review the Positioning Yourself exercise in Chapter 6, and note that each of your beliefs is just one of many components within a given area in the "Where I Am Now" column; no single one of your beliefs comprises the whole column. If you confront and handle those attitudes now, you can use them effectively to propel you toward where you want to be.

I am often asked how it's possible to get in touch with your beliefs when it's widely known that people spend long periods in therapy exploring their deep-seated attitudes. By the time most people reach this stage in the process of making dreams come true, they have little trouble voicing a wide range of attitudes and beliefs, particularly those that hold them back. Here's a roster of the ones I hear most frequently:

I don't have the time, the money, the resources, the
    skills, or the knowledge.
I'm not successful enough or not good enough.

I'm too successful, too young, too old, or too resistant to
    change.
I'm in the wrong geographical location.
I don't have any knowledge in that area.
I missed my opportunity years ago.
My energy is too low.
It's too hard or too technical for me.
I don't think I can learn what I need to know.
I don't trust myself or anyone else.
I worry about what others will think.
I don't believe it's possible, so why bother?

In an uneven economy, this is the attitude I hear expressed most
often: "I don't have enough money to do it."

I ask, "How much do you need?"

The most common answer is "I don't know, but I know I don't
have enough."

Not having enough may be a reality, but it's also a limiting
belief. There are usually creative alternatives for handling this
issue. Frequently, however, the very people who express reserva-
tions based on their finances are the ones who can't afford to stay
where they are. From an economic perspective, they would benefit from making a change.

Real People: CAROLL

When Caroll first heard me speak at a leadership retreat, she said,
"I want to come to Dream University®, but I can't afford it." Then
she angrily declared that she was sick of hearing herself say those
words.

The next thing she said surprised us both: "I'm coming to Dream
U. I don't know how I will afford it, but it's time for a breakthrough

in my life around money." She asked me to be on her DreamTeam. "Fine. Call me in a week with your credit card number."

I *do* have the time, the money, the resources, the skills, the knowledge.

I'm successful enough and good enough.

I'm old enough, young enough, and flexible enough.

I'm in a good geographical location.

I can accomplish my dream anywhere.

I have sufficient knowledge in this new area.

I have a good opportunity before me now.

My energy is high.

I believe in myself.

I can learn what I need to know.

I have no worries about what others will think

I believe my dream is possible.

She called me the next day. She had received a financial statement in the mail. One of her bonds was losing money, so she decided to sell it. Then she had enough money to pay her tuition in full and to cover her airfare to that particular retreat, which was to be held in Maui.

Caroll came to the workshop, and over and over she kept seeing where she said no, where her limiting beliefs were causing her to play it safe, and where she was killing off any new possibilities. After a week of this, we rewired her internal circuitry.

When she returned home, everything appeared different, because Caroll herself had changed. Within six months her business doubled, she received a big promotion and was praised by the president of the company in front of all her colleagues. In her personal life, she decided she wanted the perfect relationship, and the person she wanted it with was herself. She spent the next year and a half learning more about herself and how to relate to others. She cultivated new friends and ultimately decided to end a marriage that no longer supported her vision. She now has a new life of freedom and joy, is good friends with her ex-husband, and is happily dating at age forty-six.

Caroll recently told me that she has never been happier. She feels totally free and is facing unlimited horizons for her career and her personal life. Releasing the burden of carrying around a boisterous doubter can free you to find your true power and essence.

The important thing about your attitudes and beliefs is how you use them. If you believe you don't have the resources to get the job done, go back to the Positioning Yourself exercise in Chapter 6 and enter that belief in the "Where I Am Now" column. If you have a long list of attitudes and beliefs, the whole catalog belongs in the "Where I Am Now" column, whether the beliefs are positive or negative. In fact, interpreting something as a "good attitude" or a "bad attitude" doesn't make it good or bad. It's just an interpretation.

Do your beliefs empower or impede you? One day while working out at my health club, I saw Greg, a handsome man of about age thirty-eight. He was staring off into space.

I jokingly said, "C'mon, aren't you here to work out? Get going!"

He said he was thinking about the year ahead and about some goals he had set.

"Like what?" I asked.

"I plan to be walking by the end of this year," he replied, as he crawled off a Nautilus machine and reached for a wheelchair that I hadn't noticed. He explained that he was in the wrong place at the wrong time, got caught in some crossfire, and was shot in the leg. His doctors considered it a miracle that he had lived through the night. They told him and his family that he would never walk again.

However, one day while Greg lay in a hospital bed pondering the futility of his situation, his toe moved. The doctors assured him it was nothing, just nerves; but for Greg it was the beginning of a new belief. The expectation that he would walk again became the driving force of Greg's life, and he became passionately committed to turning his dream into a reality.

I saw Greg recently. Not only was he walking, but he was eager to share his new dream. "My next step is to find a girlfriend and take her dancing. But my five-year goal is to run a marathon." He chuckled. "Pretty unbelievable for a guy who was told he would never walk again."

Whose beliefs are you buying? What's stopping you from going for your dreams? Anything and everything you want is no more than a belief away.

INTERPRETATIONS

When something happens in any kind of situation, the results can be interpreted negatively or positively. Interpretation depends on attitudes and beliefs.

If a member of your staff suddenly seems to be doing unsatisfactory work, you could interpret this as the employee's lack of interest and general unhappiness. On the other hand, maybe the employee is dealing with a problem at home or is concerned about job stability. Which interpretation is correct? In this case you can avoid inaccurate interpretations by communicating with the employee. Ask the employee what's going on. Create a dialogue so you don't have to guess the reasons behind someone else's behavior.

You use interpretations to empower you by getting accurate information and by thinking of outcomes in positive terms. Possibilities will appear everywhere if you believe there are opportunities in everything that happens. If your attitude is "I'll believe it when I see it," chances are you'll never see it. This is an important point; don't glide over it!

Interpreting an attitude as

"good" or "bad"

doesn't make it good or bad;

it's just an interpretation.

Here's how your beliefs can empower or impede you in moving toward your dream. If your beliefs are obstacles, they will trip you up or keep you from stepping out into your dream. However, if you use your beliefs as tools to help you achieve your dreams, you transform them into stepping-stones. Now your beliefs have become the bridge that allows you to move easily from where you are to where you want to be. You decide. Will you use your beliefs as barriers or stepping-stones? How you see and use them is up to you. If you believe in yourself and your dreams, you'll be training yourself to use the power of interpretation to get what you want.

FACING FEAR

Imagine that there's a gift in your life, one that's so obvious that every time it shows up it's a direct sign that you're on the right path to getting what you want. Fear can be this gift, and this is how it works.

Everyone's life is about change. Sometimes *you* change, and sometimes circumstances around you change. Often when you think you have everything figured out, something happens, and the course you were on is forever altered.

As a sign on a tip jar in my local coffee shop said, "If you fear change, leave it here." Don't we wish it could be that easy? The truth seems to be that some people fear change, some people resist change, and some people claim to thrive on it. Human beings seem devoted to consistency as a way of life. Yet the only constant is change. What you fear may not revolve around what is being changed; what you call fear and associate with a negative belief may be your body's resistance to the act of changing.

When our first parents were

driven out of Paradise, Adam

is believed to have remarked to Eve,

"My dear, we live in an age of transition."

—W. C. INGE

You can learn whether you're on the right path to where you want to be by facing fear and acknowledging it as a landmark for change. That's the gift. If you were not moving away from your current identity, if you were not seeking to change your life, you would not be experiencing fear.

Because we think of change as filled with murky unknowns, the ultimate fear may feel like death. However, the experience is actually the old you dying away and allowing you to be transformed. This is good news. By trusting what you want, you will often be able to release the part of you that was afraid of making your dream come true. By shedding the parts of yourself that no longer fit, you can create a new dream to move toward. Fear is actually a measurement tool; it means that you're leaving the old behind; it's a gift that indicates you are closer to your dream.

What would you attempt

to do if you knew

you could not fail?

—DR. ROBERT SCHULLER

EMPOWERING YOURSELF OUT OF FEAR

Fear can be seen as a healthy and natural mechanism, a sign of vitality, and evidence that you are in process. Sadly, however, unless you learn to use fear to empower yourself, it also stop your progress dead in its tracks.

First you need to distinguish fear that protects from fear that restricts. When fear keeps you out of dark alleys at two o'clock in the morning, you should listen to your inner voice. On the other hand, fear of change, fear of moving closer to a dream, or fear of something that you've always wanted is negative and limiting.

Suppose you always wanted a little country home. You've dreamed about the rooms, the yard, the picket fence. One day you find your dream home and you think, "Oh, Lord, now what?" The thoughts that fly through your mind create fear, and you invent stories to justify being afraid.

"I can't give up my friends and move away."
"I'll never sell my house."
"The country home is too small (or too large) for me."
"The commute is too far."
"No one will visit me out there."
"The country house was only a dream anyway."

If you see opportunities

in everything that happens,

possibilities appear everywhere.

Take a fresh look at the dream. Start by closing your eyes and imagining your dream house. Assume there are no limiting circumstances like the ones listed above. Now ask, "Is this the house of my dreams?" If the answer is no, you can let it go. If the answer is yes, then go for it.

It's actually possible to use fear as a way of getting something that you want. Let's catch up with Ilene, whose story began in Chapter 1, to learn how she used fear to launch her dream of running her own dance company.

You may think that Ilene's experience is too neat an ending to her story, but that's just a limiting belief. Maybe you know about someone who's afraid and is unable to devise a powerful or simple solution. Having a belief means wanting the situation to turn out a certain way, and fear is often used to justify the outcome.

No matter how the situation concludes, what matters is the meaning you give to the outcome. Will a negative result mean that you're a failure and that you shouldn't go for your dream, or will you be able to accept the outcome, whatever it is? I hope you won't use the demise of a dream to stop dreaming altogether. Accepting the consequences, good or bad, will free you.

THIS SPACE IS

AVAILABLE FOR

YOUR DREAMS.

Take a risk, but be aware that things sometimes turn out differently than you expected. In Ilene's case, facing her fear enabled her to deal with it. If her plan had not worked out, she would have developed another; confronting her fear was empowering.

THOUGHTS AND FEELINGS

Earlier I mentioned that attitudes and beliefs lead to thoughts and feelings, which in turn lead to decisions and choices. If you want to become aware of your attitudes and beliefs, remember to pay attention to what you're thinking and feeling.

If your dream is to establish a new career but your belief is that it's not possible, what do you think and feel about that? Do you feel futility? Are you resigned to the idea that you can't have your dream? Or do you think you can have what you want because you deserve it?

Suppose your dream is to be famous. Specifically, you want the *New York Times* to write a front-page story about you, but you don't believe it's possible. The logical sequence of your thought process might be that you don't think it can happen so you decide not even to pursue it.

Now you have the same dream with a different belief. You believe it's possible to make your dream come true. Here is your

Keep speaking your dream.

Keep speaking the possibility.

thought process: "I think I can make this happen," and "I think I know who can help me." Your new choice is to go for it.

Simply changing your belief has shifted your internal conversation from thinking of your dream as impossible to seeing its possibilities. This is an example of removing the obstacles in order to let the opportunities occur.

Real People: ILENE

Ilene, who wanted to become the full-time executive director of her own dance company, feared severing her ties with the people at her current place of employment. She'd worked there for a long time and had developed relationships that mattered to her. She believed that if she left, the relationships would end. That belief was somehow turned into a fear that she was going to be alone in her new venture.

When Ilene clarified where she wanted to be, she decided to take her relationships with her. She also realized that one of her skills—writing grant proposals in the field of the arts—was something she could sell to the company for which she'd been working.

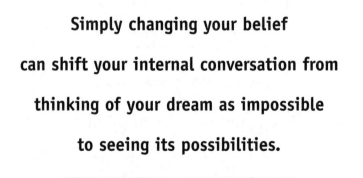

Simply changing your belief

can shift your internal conversation from

thinking of your dream as impossible

to seeing its possibilities.

Ilene approached her employer and suggested that his company become Ilene's client. Her employer, seeing the value in hiring someone on a project-by-project basis, accepted Ilene's proposal. Because she assumed a new role, that of freelancer, the project was awarded to Ilene on her own terms. She negotiated more money, better hours, and greater flexibility than she'd had as the company's employee. Without announcing her fears, Ilene was able to use them as a mechanism for getting her employer to become her client. It is important to notice that Ilene identified her fears to herself and developed a way to deal with them that catapulted her dream into reality.

Ilene also saw that she had been using her fear for a long time to stop herself from moving forward. There was a gap between where she was and where she wanted to be and that gap was created by her beliefs. When she examined her attitudes honestly, she was able to use them to break through and move toward what she wanted. In fact, she wound up with more than she thought she could have: she didn't just walk away from her employer feeling okay about it; she walked away with a new client and a powerful relationship with her former boss.

You will find it easier to become aware of your thoughts and feelings now that you're clear about your attitudes and beliefs. It's even possible, once you understand that you have a core belief, to go back and change it. If you alter your beliefs, your thoughts and feelings will change, too. Your changed thoughts and feelings, in turn, will motivate you to examine your decisions and choices. What decisions are you making in your life? Are they positive choices that will move you toward your dream, or are your decisions moving you away from things you want?

This point is so important that I want to illustrate it again. We often think we know who will or won't help us and who will give us flak on our dreams. However, we may be surprised.

Real People: RENEE

Renee was the marketing director for one of the premier motor-cycle events in the world, but her dream was to publish a quarterly magazine covering the top motorcycle rallies in the United States.

She described her dream to the sales manager of the *Sturgis Rally News* magazine and, concerned about jeopardizing her current position, asked that he keep her dream confidential. Lucky for Renee, he did not honor her request. Instead, he told the owner of the magazine about her dream. Little did she know that the owner's dream was to diversify his company and publish more magazines.

When you identify your fears

and learn to use them positively,

you can develop ways to deal with them

that will catapult your dream into reality.

Renee was hired to launch the new magazine, and since her dream included not moving, because of her son, she is managing this new publication from her hometown (200 miles from the company's main location). They just formed the Motorcycle Events Association, which her new boss financed. This was a dream come true. Because she shared her dream, it became even bigger and more wonderful than she had imagined.

Perhaps your dream is to move from the East Coast to the West Coast or from California to New York, but you fear that such a move would put you too far away from your family. That fear may arise from a belief that your family won't love you if they don't see you. Is this belief real? This is a good question to ask yourself about all your beliefs, because the truth is that beliefs are not real. They are something we have created, and we have the power to revise or replace them at any time.

You can change your attitude by adopting the belief that you can have friends all over the world. The new outlook will help you understand that, wherever you're living, family and friends will come to visit you, that you can visit them, and that you'll make new friends easily. Thus, you have adopted a positive feeling about yourself and your place in the world. Then, if you decide, as I did, to move to California, the choice will be easy.

Some people think it's difficult to change a belief, and other people think it's easy; that's just your belief about your beliefs. If you have a belief that is getting in your way and is crying out to be changed, The Big Book of Your Beliefs exercise can help you do it.

Your attitudes and beliefs can empower you or frustrate you. By confronting doubt and fear, you will allow opportunity to show up. But the door is closed where doubt reigns. You need to believe—in yourself and in your dreams. Then you can make decisions and choices that support making your dreams come true.

THE BIG BOOK OF YOUR BELIEFS

Find a quiet spot and relax. Take several deep breaths and prepare yourself for a journey. Imagine that you're in the attic of your mind. It's filled with lots of dusty memories: your bicycle from when you were ten, your mother's wedding dress, old photo albums.

In one corner of the attic is a beautiful pedestal on which rests a big book entitled *My Beliefs*. Blow a little dust off the book, open it, and turn to a page where you have a belief that you want to change.

See your belief on that page. You can write in the space below or just picture it in your mind. Whatever that old belief is, read it, and prepare to change it.

My limiting belief that is stopping me from having my dream come true is:

_____

_____

_____

Perhaps you believe it's not possible to have what you want. Read that belief from the page in the book, take a big black marker and draw a huge X through it. Then tear the page out of the book and burn it. Feel the emotion of finally letting this old belief go.

Now you're left with a clean page in the book, because there was nothing behind the page you tore out. Pick up a new marker pen in your favorite color and write your new belief. Your new belief will correspond to the one you destroyed, but it will be stated positively and in the first person: "It is possible for me to have what I want." Consider adding the word "easily."

Write your new belief expressively and with a flair, so that you feel it and can internalize it. After you've written it, read your new belief out loud to yourself. Then close the book, leave the attic, and know that your new, positive attitude now lives in the big book of your beliefs.

My wonderful new belief is:

_____

_____

_____

Do you believe you changed your belief? Do you believe that it's at least possible you changed it? Or do you believe it can't be that easy? What if it is that easy? It's all up to you. You decide whether to believe or not. That's how beliefs work.

CHAPTER 8

The "C" Word: Commitment

Never, never, never, never give up.

—SIR WINSTON CHURCHILL

NOW THAT YOU HAVE DETERMINED where you are and where you want to be, you'll have to make a choice. Do you feel a greater commitment to having more of the same or to making your dream come true?

Many of the people I coach find that, once they get to the commitment stage, dramatic things happen. Some of the Real People stories at the end of this chapter illustrate not only how people move into the commitment stage but how their dream happens once the commitment is made.

An important question to ask is what kind of commitment you're willing to make to achieve your dream. The answer may surprise you, just as the Carters were surprised that they wanted to close the business to which they thought they were devoted. However, once you are committed to making your dream come true, everything seems to move faster, and you seem to know with greater certainty how you need to proceed. Your next step becomes evident, as does the step after that.

Until one is committed, there is hesitancy, the chance to draw back, always ineffectiveness, concerning all acts of initiative (and creation). There is one elementary truth the ignorance of which kills countless ideas and splendid plans: that the moment one definitely commits oneself, then providence moves too. All sorts of things occur to help one that would never otherwise have occurred. A whole stream of events issues from the decision, raising in one's favor all manner of unforeseen incidents and meetings and material assistance which no one could have dreamed would have come their way. Whatever you can do or dream you can, begin it. Boldness has *genius, power,* and *magic* in it. Begin it now.

—JOHANN WOLFGANG VON GOETHE

I sometimes refer to commitment as the "C" word because a lot of people think of it as if it were an obscenity. Perhaps they view commitment as being locked in or as being stuck.

When I speak of commitment, I mean a covenant with yourself and for yourself; committing to something that you want, to making your dream come true, to moving forward. "Commitment" is not a dirty word; on the contrary, it's a powerful experience.

Nevertheless there are some common attitudes and beliefs that stop people from making a commitment to themselves:

"Making a choice is going to force my hand."
"I'll be stuck with my decision and won't be able to
     change direction later."
"This might be the wrong move and, if I keep my options
     open, something better will show up."
"I might look silly.
"Getting there will take too long."
"I might not be able to do what I say."
"I might not be able to follow through."
"What if I fail?"

You can deal with commitment in a manner similar to the way you treated fear in Chapter 7: you can redefine "commitment" as something positive, a tool that you can use to propel yourself toward having your dream. Maybe what you've always needed to reach your dream was to have two thousand dollars; commit to accumulating that sum by a certain date so you can put yourself into action. Commitment is a much more powerful way of living than waiting around and hoping or, worse, never doing anything to make your dreams happen.

"Moving forward is going to open up

new possibilities."

"I am choosing what I want.

Life is full of choices."

"Taking action might be a good move,

and if I stay committed other good things

will show up."

"It won't take long for me to get there."

"I may do exactly what I say."

"I will be able to follow through."

"I intend to succeed."

WALK YOUR TALK

A critical element of commitment is doing what you say you're going to do, actually being as good as your word—walking your talk.

Right now your dream doesn't exist in reality. It begins to take on life as you envision it and speak about it. During the commitment stage, as you open yourself up to new possibilities, many things can start to happen. If you're not responsible for your commitment, the process will start to unravel and you will undermine yourself and your dream. Get into the practice of following through on your commitment: walk your talk. Maintain your integrity.

When you make a commitment, a new dynamic will show up, bringing opportunities you didn't know were possible. Be especially careful at this point to avoid being stopped by limiting beliefs and attitudes; sometimes in the commitment phase self-sabotage can sneak up on you when you're least expecting it.

I was so excited about taking my dream holiday in Greece. I had my ticket and a place to stay and I was committed. So why when a client called me with a big job, to take place right smack in the middle of my planned trip, did I accept the job, which would mean cutting my vacation time in half? That evening I was grumpy to the people I love, and I became suspicious that something was going on, something that I was not aware of. Then it hit me: I was selling out on my own dream. Integrity means keeping your agreements with yourself too, perhaps especially with yourself. The next day I called my client and apologized, telling her I would not be able to speak at her event. "Why?" she had to ask. I took a deep breath, and for a moment, was concerned about what she would think of me. "I'm going to Greece to pursue a long-deferred dream. I'm sorry."

"Why would you be sorry?" my client said. "I'm just sorry I'm not going with you. We'll try to schedule you to speak at our conference next year."

These sabotaging patterns can be subtle. For example, you might be committed to doing something even though you're worried about not having the time or money to do it. Don't give up because of your concern. By acting on your commitment, you open up opportunities—perhaps some new resource that will make the whole thing feasible. You might say that, if you are willing to make the commitment down to the marrow in your bones, amazing things will happen in your life, and wonderful people will appear to help you. This is not about being flaky or irresponsible. Say yes to what you want, even if it takes you into foreign territory.

The Sliding Glass Door exercise on page 108 will help you learn to live in your commitment. When you have completed the exercise, you may decide not to commit and step through the door. That's fine. Be clear that this side of the glass door is where you choose to be right now. Your dream will always be there on the other side of the sliding glass door. When you are ready, you can reach out, open the door, and step through.

Real People: THE CARTERS

The Carters, the couple who owned their own store, were committed to having a successful business. They were surprised to learn that their retail operation, to which they had been devoted, was not the kind of success they wanted.

When they understood that where they were wasn't even close to where they wanted to be, the Carters realized that they had to make a decision: did they want more of the same, or were they ready to make a commitment to having their dream? When they decided to live on purpose and move forward with their dream, they did so in a big way. They closed their store and transformed their whole business, to say nothing of their lives, into something else.

Because amazing things happen when we commit, changes started to occur for the Carters. When they recognized how central their relationship was to each of them, they committed to creating a shared goal out of their individual purposes. The unexpected outcome of all this was that they became more committed to each other.

The Carters' commitment got them into immediate action. Within three months they had phased out of their retail operation and created a new consulting business that gave them greater flexibility and the opportunity to work in closer partnership with each other. Their commitment catapulted them into an even bigger and much better dream.

THE SLIDING GLASS DOOR

Remove yourself from distractions by finding a place where you won't be disturbed. Relax. Take a few deep breaths. This exercise is completely about you, about stepping into your commitment.

Imagine that you're standing with your nose pressed against a glass door, so close to it that your breath is steaming up the glass. When you wipe away the steam, you see a beautiful place on the other side of the glass. Rainbows, waterfalls, animals, heaven on earth.

Feel your feet standing on the floor on your side of the glass door, the other side of your dream world. You're standing in the "Where I Am Now," where you live with everything that's happening in your life, including your attitudes and beliefs. Looking through the glass door, you can see the beauty on the other side. You will have the opportunity to find out if the other side is a place where you want to be.

Grasp the handle and slide the door open. A gentle breeze wafts in, and there's a delicious smell in the air. You feel warm and welcomed.

As you gaze around, you see everything on the other side that you want, everything that's in your dream, everything you're committed to having: your family is there, your friends, your dream house, your dream life. All the elements of your dream are there, on the other side of the door.

Notice where you are and where you want to be. All you need to do to get to the other side is make the commitment and step through.

Ask yourself, "Is this what I want? Will I commit to this?" If the answer is yes, lift your foot and step through.

Now you're on the other side, living in a land of possibilities. Here's where all your dreams can come true. Don't worry if you don't have it all figured out. Just trust: now that you're standing in your commitment, you're standing in your dream.

Take a couple of deep breaths and relax. Now rate your passion level. It will probably be quite high. Good work!

PASSION SCALE

Place an X next to the term that best describes your level of passion about your commitment. Do it right now.

____ Red hot
____ Turned on
____ Excited
____ Very interested
____ Interested
____ Some possibility
____ No interest

Real People: NANCY

Nancy, the woman who started a new business while she was pregnant with her first baby, was committed to having balance in her life. For Nancy, that meant having quality time for her husband and baby and also for her new business.

The issue wasn't about only balancing time; it also was about balancing energy so she would have enough to give to both areas of her life. Nancy's commitment was to be the best that she could be personally and professionally, without selling out on herself.

Everybody has only twenty-four hours in each day, and Nancy began to think about how she was going to use the allotted time to achieve her dream. Once she understood her commitment clearly, the steps she needed to take became obvious.

Nancy decided that she was going to work only a certain number of days each week. She built a lot of flexibility into that decision by allowing herself to choose weekly which days that would be. She did not see her overall commitment to her business as amorphous, but she allowed herself to be accommodating in the way she made it work.

She also knew she would need some help to achieve the flexibility she wanted, and she immediately hired a live-in housekeeper. That relieved her both of the concern about child care while she was at the office and of the need to perform household chores. Thus, when Nancy came home from her new business, she had the time and energy to be with her family. Her commitment to her dreams enabled her to create a balanced life, one that she freely chose and loved living.

If this kind of luxury seems impossible on of your budget, maybe you can enter into a barter arrangement with students seeking housing. Commitment comes in many different forms. Get creative. Success is up to you.

Commitment leads to action

and action brings your dream closer.

CHAPTER 9

Yes, It's Possible— A Rallying Cry

You see things; and you say, "Why?"
But I dream things that never were; and I say, "Why not?"
—GEORGE BERNARD SHAW

WE BEGAN THIS BOOK speaking about possibility as something you can have. In this chapter, you get to play with your dream as if you truly believe it's possible to have what you're committed to, to have all the goals in your life align, to have a life you love, to have the time to enjoy it, and to start right now. Check in with yourself. Does this sound enticing or frightening?

I am talking about being open to a world of possibilities. Having possibility in your life requires that you practice at every opportunity to speak the words, "It is possible," and to believe them. Unfortunately, most of us have been trained to believe that the things we want are not possible. To change that takes retraining. You can learn to hear yourself, and you can educate those around you to hear the possibility in what you say, instead of "Have you gone mad?"

The assumption that it is possible is at the core of having your dream come true. If you have read this far in the book and you confess that you don't believe you can have your dream, then you should confront and handle your negative beliefs before you go on. You may wish to go back and read some of the earlier chapters to identify what's holding you back and how you can change it. You can't make your dream come true if you don't believe it's possible.

The Sliding Glass Door exercise in Chapter 8 is one method you can employ here. On this side of the door is your belief that your dream is not possible, but on the other side are many possibilities. Notice where you're standing. Are you on this side, in "I don't believe it's possible," or are you on the other side, standing in your commitment? Choose one.

You can suspend your negative attitude and say, "I'll believe it for a while and give it a shot." However, I recommend that you walk through that door. Be committed to making your dream come true, be willing to have it be possible, allow your attitudes and beliefs to support you, and stop holding on to outdated negative opinions. Step through the doorway; that's where the surprises will happen. Being open to possibility means you are open to hope, and hope invites us to say yes to life. From here you will have many opportunities to deal with your concerns and to move you to the next step.

MOVING INTO YOUR PROJECTS

Possibility begins to seem likely when you move forward from dreams to projects. As you start to involve yourself in the specific results, the dream will become animated and take on credibility. If you don't know how to accomplish that, relax; we'll explore ways to make it happen.

When you've made your commitment, you will have a different perspective on your dream than you did when you were wondering if it would ever happen. Maybe you once thought you didn't have the time to go after that new piece of business that you want; now that you're committed to doing it, and you've dealt with all your negative attitudes and beliefs, you may see the logic of freeing time by giving up something that doesn't interest you anymore. Your new outlook—that it makes sense to give up something that no longer has value to you—is a direct result of your ability to see where you are, compared to where you want to be. If there is something you don't have to do and don't want to do, why are you doing it? The most common reason surely is guilt. By creating dreams that include the people you love and care about, you can avoid negative and destructive feelings.

Your dream is possible.

Refocusing on your life's purpose (who you are and what turns you on) will help you decide when to give up or walk away from something. You'll notice a lighter, freer feeling as you let go of the old and create room to embrace the new.

Living up to your commitments also allows you to form new relationships and to connect resources in creative ways that you hadn't considered before. You don't yet have to focus on the specific strategies and steps; look at what else you might put into your dream to have everything you want. Your commitment may even lead you to include items you didn't know about earlier.

For example, in defining your dream now, you might say, "I want an understanding, industrious, supportive partner." Or "I will find a venture capitalist who's interested in funding my project." Perhaps you're ready to brainstorm with other people; now that you see your dream clearly and you're committed to having it, you can discuss it with a group of individuals whom you respect and who can help you decide on the specifics.

Maybe you have already determined that you want to live in a particular location, and now you want to put some flesh on the bare bones of that dream: a particular kind of house, a pool or Jacuzzi, walk-in closets for your designer wardrobe. Have fun with this while you allow your dream to grow.

New possibilities will also appear when you create balance in your life. You begin to see, as Nancy did, that you can be successful in business and still have time to spend with your family. You'll also see that, once you set aside your negative attitudes and beliefs, you can allow yourself to hire somebody to cook dinner or to make your life easier in some other way.

The smartest thing I think I have ever done was to hire a personal chef. I contacted the Association of Personal Chefs and found Jeff Parrott. Every two weeks he comes to my home, bringing with him pots and pans, food and spices, storage containers and labels. He spends five hours in my kitchen cooking up a storm. The smells are so wonderful I usually come begging for a snack, which he always graciously prepares. Although I am welcome to hang out with him and get some culinary lessons, I am much more interested in the end product. He hands me my menu for the coming weeks and fills my freezer with healthy gourmet entrées, side dishes, soups, and snacks. I am in heaven. All week long I eat well, I can have people over and impress them (although I always give credit to Jeff), and I have no pans to

WHAT ELSE IS POSSIBLE?

DO NOT SKIP THIS EXERCISE. When you think you've listed every-thing that's possible and you're sure there's nothing left, ask yourself again, "What else is possible?" I assure you more will come.

What else is possible? _____

_____

_____

_____

What else is possible? _____

_____

_____

_____

What else is possible? _____

_____

_____

_____

What else is possible? _____

_____

_____

_____

wash. These meals wind up being cheaper and much less fatten-
ing than eating out every night. I highly recommend hiring a personal chef.

The important question, now and always, is, "What else is possible?" At the end of this chapter you will find the continuing
story of the Carters, who found many possibilities once they
began to live in their commitment. Nancy, the expectant mother
with the new business, discovered such possibilities as working
fewer days and hiring live-in help. For Ilene, the woman who
started the dance company, the possibilities were to write grant
proposals as a freelancer, to provide other consulting services,
and to raise sponsorship dollars for her new venture.

On page 115 you will find an exercise that will help you ask
yourself, "What else is possible?" Do not skip this exercise. It will
help to ensure that you have included in your dream all the
aspects or details you truly want.

The Looking Back exercise will also help you see what else is
possible. In your mind's eye project yourself ahead one year.
Looking back from that point, write out how the last year was for
you. Remember who you are now: someone standing in your life's
purpose, whose dreams are deliberately chosen, who has a clear
sense of where you are and where you want to be, and who has
removed all limiting beliefs and obstacles.

Through the Looking Back exercise you can develop a game
plan by projecting yourself into the future to look back at the
past. You can also understand the feelings and sensations of those
events that are *about* to unfold in your life. Because you have
become so focused and directed, the high probability is that, over
the next year, you will live out your projection. Your dreams will
come true.

Be specific when you're looking back. State your accomplishments during the last year. Draw the complete picture for your-

self, leaving out none of the details. Remember, you stepped through the sliding door.

What were you passionate about?

Where did your achievements take place?

Who else was involved?

What funds became available?

How did you spend the extra money that came your way?

How did others respond?

How did you feel as you passed certain milestones?

How did going down one path take you to another?

Whom did you meet this year that you always wanted to meet?

How did you spend your vacation?

How did you look and feel?

How was that last year for you, now that you made your dream come true?

LOOKING BACK

How this year was for me (if everything was possible):

_____

_____

_____

_____

_____

_____

_____

_____

_____

_____

_____

_____

_____

_____

_____

_____

_____

Let more and more come to you as you're writing; you'll be surprised at how much detail you will have about the "past" year. Make it up exactly as you want it to be. Do not compromise here.

Everything up to this point—all the exercises, visualizations, writings—has been a projection of what you want to have. Now we will transform it all into projects with specific results. This is where all your dreams will begin to become part of your reality, and where your passion will ignite your dreams.

Real People: THE CARTERS

The Carters began to see the possibilities as soon as they made their commitment to sell the retail computer store and pursue their dreams. First, they realized they could develop a whole new consulting business serving clients with whom they had done business before. Second, they determined that they could sell their retail business to someone who would continue to serve their previous customers. Third, they could ask the new owner to send them the retail customers who needed consultation about purchases made at the store.

In other words, they took their dream to a new level by developing a new relationship. Instead of separating themselves completely from their previous business, they found a way to make a profitable connection for their new business.

Wasn't this coming year a great year?

Of course, they had to overcome some obstacles. The Carters had many attitudes and beliefs about closing the store. They couldn't see how they were going to continue serving their clients, for example, and they thought that closing the store meant they had failed. You need to understand that changing your mind, or even failing at a dream, does not mean you are a failure.

Once they went through their process, the Carters were able to turn their negative attitudes and beliefs around, and use them to propel themselves toward their dream. When they knew with clarity what they wanted, and when they were committed to having it, the next steps became evident: they scheduled the closing of the store, they set a date by which the new business would be set up, and they got into action. Setting the date made the commitment tangible and moved their dream into the project phase, the subject of the next chapter.

All that we see or seem

is but a dream within a dream.

—EDGAR ALLAN POE

CHAPTER 10

Projects That Move You Forward

If you have built castles in the air,
your work need not be lost; that is where they should be.
Now put the foundations under them.

—HENRY DAVID THOREAU

IN CHAPTER 4 YOU CHOSE a specific area of your life to work on, to simplify the process of learning the techniques in this book. You've been developing your dream in that area, going up the Passion Pyramid, opening up more and more possibilities about your dream. In this chapter you will learn how to turn your dream into a project with specific, measurable results. The act of doing so will make your dream begin to exist in your life, not just in your head or on paper.

Remember that everything comes from purpose. Standing in your purpose, ask, with respect to the area you selected, "What dream do I have that I can turn into an exciting project?" Then look for what you need to add to your project to get it scheduled into your life—a date, a person, a number.

For instance, if your dream is to travel, your project might be to go on a vacation this year. If you don't yet know where you want to go, but you know that you want an exotic locale, open an atlas, pick a specific place, and begin to plan your trip.

Dreams come alive through projects

with specific and measurable results.

My own life's purpose is to joyously self-express, and my personal dream is to travel the world in style and elegance; my project is to book an exotic cruise by a specific date.

Of course, there are many ways to travel the world in style and elegance. Other projects that could come from my purpose and my dream might be to travel first class five times this year; to attend at least three formal events in cities outside my hometown; to fly in a private jet plane at least once during the next six months; to spend three months in a foreign country living in a beautiful place.

You don't have to limit yourself to one project; all you have to do is make sure that your projects move you forward toward your dream. When I develop projects for my professional dream—integrating more leisure time into my work—I can change things around, as long as everything remains aligned with my purpose and my professional dream. Thus I might create a project that would allow me to continue my work while taking in the California scenery. Note that I only have to create the project at this point; I don't have to limit the possibilities by figuring out how I'm going to do it. Going to strategy too soon can sometimes kill your passion. We'll get to the planning process shortly.

Ellen, whose purpose was to have a life filled with fun and adventure, had as a well-being goal "to live a spa life." Her project was to go to an elegant spa for at least a week four times a year. She didn't yet have any of it planned—financially, logistically, or time-wise—but once she created the project, it took on life and became part of her reality.

Some projects are easy; you merely have to schedule them into your calendar: to get into action on her dream, Ellen developed a simple project to get two facials and two massages each month. Since I too love the idea of a "spa life," I was inspired by her dream and adopted it as one of my own. I now lead one of my Dream University® retreats at a world-class spa. You can join me for hiking, facials, massages, and in-depth dream work.

If you want your dreams to come true, don't sleep.

—YIDDISH PROVERB

Some projects can be just that simple while others are complicated and require a well-thought-out plan. A project has to be specific, but it can deal with any aspect of your life: Brian created a plan to raise $25,000 so his company could open for business in a big way. The only two criteria for a project are that it come from the bottom up on the Passion Pyramid—meaning that it's an expression of your purpose and your dream—and that it be specific and measurable.

SYNCHRONICITY

Synchronicity may be a fun, new way for you to think about having your dream. Before reading this book, perhaps you thought about your dream as something that might or might not come true. Now you've expanded your possibilities and allowed for more opportunities to create projects for reaching your dream. I gave a speech in Madrid to the Young Presidents' Organization. At the end of my talk a lovely woman with a beautiful European accent asked me to share one of my dreams with her. I thought to myself, "Take a risk. There must be an opportunity at hand." I told her that my dream was to spend the summer in Greece writing a novel. She opened her purse and handed me a business card, saying, "I have a villa in Greece and it's empty all summer. Please come as my guest." And I did. Every day, my belief that magic happens when you share your dream, is validated.

When you look at the whole picture of your dream, you will see that some of the areas may overlap, providing shortcuts. Or the overlap will enable you to handle something in one area of your life that automatically takes care of something in another area. This is called synchronicity: when things happen at the right time, when they flow together easily and work interchangeably. This synchronicity creates ease. In order to have more of this, you must practice integrity. Say what you mean, mean what you say, and trust that you can easily make your dreams come true.

People will call me and say, "I followed the process, I did all the steps, but I keep having setbacks." When I ask them about their life, their relationships, their agreements with others and themselves, I often find that they are saying one thing and doing another. Everything we say, do, think, feel, and are affects everything we want and have. Notice how you are in your life. Perhaps take a personal inventory and pay extra attention to what you are saying and doing. When we have integrity life seems to just ebb and flow and we have greater ease. If life is taking you on a bumpy ride it may be a message to check in and see how you are living.

If you stand in your purpose and look at the broad picture of your dream, it's possible to get what you want while simplifying your life. New possibilities will become available as you develop projects and get into action on them. Opportunities that you couldn't have seen before will start to look as if they have potential. Of course, an old attitude or belief might stymie you. If this happens, ask yourself whether you're still committed to your dream. If the answer is yes, do something. Take some small step to demonstrate your commitment.

Synchronicity:

when things happen at the right time,

flow together easily

and work interchangeably.

You have no idea what could be waiting for you right around the bend, on the other side of the place where you got stuck. As long as your projects come from your purpose and are aligned with your dreams, as long as you still feel the passion, stay in action.

Throughout this book, for the sake of simplicity, we have focused on your dreams in one area of your life. However, the goal of the process is to master the techniques of consciously designing your entire life. Once you learn the procedure—and you can learn it only by practicing—you'll be able to apply it to all the other areas of your life.

I've cleared away tremendous clutter in my home and office, but my project files remain. As they grow, they open onto more projects, and sometimes new projects develop within existing ones. There's a great deal of overlap because one of my dreams is to integrate my personal life and my professional life. That doesn't mean I'm a workaholic; it means that I've created work that expresses who I am in the world, and I can combine my work with the rest of my life, easily and joyfully.

ALIGNING GOALS TO SUPPORT YOUR DREAM

Let's recap what you've accomplished thus far. Standing in your purpose, you have created dreams in at least one aspect of your life. You've stepped through the sliding glass door and you're on the other side, where there is everything you're interested in or committed to having. Now go back and have a look at the other areas of your life to ensure that they line up with your dream.

As you create a project, if you find a dream that seems inconsistent or incompatible—perhaps you're worried that you're selling out in one situation in order to have another—check to see whether your concern is real, or whether it's a negative attitude or belief. For example, if the hours you've designated for your project add up to more than twenty-four each day, you have an inconsistency. On the other hand, if they add up to six or eight and you're still troubled about having enough time for everything, acknowledge that the issue comes from an old belief. Then make a commitment that you will use your time in support of making your dream come true.

You have no idea

what could be waiting for you

right around the bend,

on the other side

of the place where you got stuck.

Look at your life holistically; all of the components, including the dreams, should be working parts of your life. Get a picture of your life as a whole; perhaps there's a piece missing that would tie things together to give you more time and flexibility, making your life easier.

During the Sliding Glass Door exercise, one of my clients became very anxious. "I can't step through," she claimed.

When I asked why not, she explained there was no ground, no

foundation. "Well, put it in," I said. What we imagine about our dreams can reveal what we are feeling. With the foundation in place, she could step through the door.

We later saw that her dream—to make some radical changes in her business—was a big stretch from where she was. When she realized the emotional difficulty her employees were having with her new plans, she began to lay the proper groundwork with them to make a smooth transition.

What are your images and feelings telling you? What's missing from your life that, if in place, would make your life easier?

Align your dreams by

eliminating any inconsistencies.

I'm not torn between my personal and professional aspects; they are both me. I give myself plenty of time to relax and play, so when I go away on vacation I often do it in a barter situation: perhaps I offer a workshop in exchange for a week at a health spa. Trading my services takes into consideration many of my dreams: my professional dream of having work that I love and that expresses who I am in the world; my personal dream of being with creative visionaries to produce results that have an impact; my well-being dream of emotional, mental, spiritual, and physical balance. The bartering opportunities arose only after I became clear about what I wanted and what I was committed to; now they occur regularly, and they tie together many of the aspects of my life.

A question that often comes up is how you identify the area you may have missed, the very one that may give you the complete set of tools you need to make your dreams come true. Go back to the Passion Pyramid and look at your life's purpose. Then look at all the dreams you have determined you want in every aspect of your life. Ask yourself, "What would make my life easier? What would make my life take on a glow? What would give me more time, more fun, more excitement?"

This is not an exercise in creating more work for yourself. Rather, by asking yourself during the alignment process what you might not have seen before as a possibility, you will simplify your life and allow yourself to see new possibilities. A growing number of people find that what's missing is not necessarily tangible; they might need more space, more time, or some other personal resource.

What would make your life easier?

What would make your life take on a glow?

What would give you more time, more fun, more excitement?

You don't necessarily have to create another project to accomplish these things; perhaps you can save yourself time and energy by linking together two or more of the projects you've already identified. Think positively; you are designing a new life for yourself. Rather than formulating a dream that's stated in the negative, such as "Remove some of the clutter," develop instead a dream that supports your having more space, time, freedom, or flexibility:

Do you want to be more relaxed because you will feel better if you stop taking everything so seriously?
Did you plan for enough recreational time and time simply to breathe and to be?
Is there a volunteer effort or some other contribution you want to make?
Are you making space in your life for what you want?

Years ago I discovered that what was missing for me was work that I loved. Just plugging that one piece into my dream enabled me to begin developing projects I could savor. For example, it had never occurred to me before that going on a cruise or to a spa was a way of making money or being successful in business. That possibility showed up when I included the element of having work that I love, and saw that I could tie it together with my other dreams. While I was in Buffalo, New York, recently on a book tour, I visited Niagara Falls, and when I went to Cincinnati I purchased a last-minute ticket to a touring Broadway show. With a little effort, I can have fun wherever I go and not have my life be just about work or no work. I realized that I could flourish and take better care of myself while spending less time and energy than I had before, and that I could take time to play.

The more of yourself that you have, the more you can put into your projects, which are a way for you to project your dreams into the world. Schedule time for your dreams and for the things that make you happy.

You can do work that you love.

STRETCH YOURSELF

If you want to live every day with passion, design a project that's bigger than your life, one that you don't know how to accomplish. Don't create a project out of the blue; develop one out of your purpose as you would any other project. My bigger-than-life project is that, by the time I die, people will be speaking about dreams in a completely new way, as if their dreams are something that absolutely can come true by a specific day. When you speak to me about your dreams, be prepared to pull out your calendar. I'm interested in getting you into action to make your dreams come true.

I'm not yet certain how to fulfill my bigger-than-life project, but it turns me on and gets me into conversation with extraordinary people. Remember, my dream is to partner with creative visionaries to produce significant results. Speaking with people about their dreams allows each of us to become a visionary, to be turned on and excited about our ideas.

I don't allow myself to be stopped by the fact that I haven't figured out how to accomplish my bigger-than-life project. I move

The Passion Pyramid

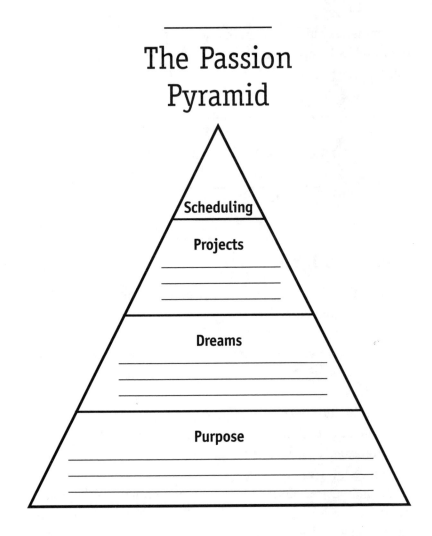

Scheduling

Projects

Dreams

Purpose

on by developing strategies and steps, by scheduling it into my life and letting life happen. And it does.

To keep yourself updated on your progress as you move up the Passion Pyramid, reenter your purpose, rewrite your dream, and indicate in the designated area on the pyramid the project you created during this chapter. Make sure you are excited about your project and the possibilities it offers.

Remember that your purpose is what turns you on; from that you created dreams that fulfill your purpose; then you developed a project or several projects to get you going on your dream. Check in by rating yourself on the Passion Scale.

If you have created something that doesn't turn you on, change it. Develop a different project. If it all lines up and you're excited and even a little nervous about how you're going to make it happen, let's move on to doing it!

PASSION SCALE

Place an X next to the term that best describes your level of passion about your project. Do it right now.

_____ Red hot
_____ Turned on
_____ Excited
_____ Very interested
_____ Interested
_____ Some possibility
_____ No interest

CHAPTER 11

Strategies and Steps— Being in Action

Divide and conquer.

—CHINESE PROVERB

NOW THAT YOU KNOW what your project is, all you have to do is figure out how to to make it happen! There are multiple ways of completing any project or achieving any end result. To make your project part of your reality, you will need strategies and steps to guide you toward your dream.

Some of us are great dreamers, but a little lacking in the strategy department. And some of us are brilliant strategists, but need a little practice dreaming. I think we should pump up both muscles, both sides of our brain. Let's dream and imagine and be practical strategists. Let's dream and make our dreams come true.

A strategy is the approach or plan you will take to actually achieve your dream. Tactics are the specific step-by-step actions taken to accomplish the strategy. Sometimes, when an entire project is put on a "to do" list, the project is actually composed of four or five separate tactics; if the separate tasks aren't listed individually, the project may never be completed. As a matter of fact, the point at which some dreams die is the moment when we put them on a "to do" list. Before you schedule a task, break it down into small steps that can be easily accomplished. Otherwise you'll probably never get to it. When you get clear about the project, as you did in the last chapter, you can explore the strategies and steps you will need to accomplish it.

For example, I decided to create a project called "Go On at Least One Free and Fun Cruise to an Exotic Place within the Next Three Months." Then I listed the ways I could make it happen. I couldn't purchase a ticket for a cruise, because my project was to go on a *free* cruise. It's important to be clear about what you want. One set of strategies might be needed to go on a fun cruise, while a different set is required to go on a *free and fun* cruise.

Other strategies I could have chosen include finding someone to pay for my trip, or entering a contest to win a free cruise. I chose to create a bartering relationship by booking my workshop on a cruise ship in return for a free trip.

The steps to accomplish the strategy were clear: list and describe some topics about which I could speak; prepare a biography; get the names and numbers of several cruise ship lines that might be interested in such an arrangement. I decided to focus my energy on a certain cruise ship, rather than mass-mailing my proposal: I wanted the best cruise I could find, so I committed to getting booked by Cunard Lines, which owns the luxury liner *Queen Elizabeth II*.

Because I was passionate about what I was doing, I felt powerful about accomplishing my goal. I was definitely in action. In three weeks, I developed promotional materials, had a photo made, sent out a package, and scheduled a date by which I wanted to set sail. Before I had a chance to make a follow-up call to see if Cunard was interested, they called me. I was booked to go on the cruise five months ahead of what I had scheduled.

A man's real worth is determined

by what he does when he has nothing to do.

—MEGIDDO MESSAGE

If I can make this kind of thing happen, so can you. On the following pages you will find forms you can use to develop the strategies and steps you will need to create your own projects and make your dreams come true. Follow the simple directions for designing a blueprint, and walk through the process.

DESIGNING A BLUEPRINT

Here is a formula for getting into action on any project:

1. Outline what you need. Use the Strategies and Steps form on page 138.
2. Break the steps down into single tasks.
3. Identify your resources. Be creative.
4. Add dates and resources.
5. Put your tasks in chronological order, using the Scheduling form on page 139.
6. See where you are overscheduled and where you can reschedule.
7. Be in action on your dream every day or at least every week.

BEING RESOURCEFUL

When you create successful strategies and steps, it is crucial to make use of the resources in all the areas of your life. List yours on the form on page 140. Think about the people you know in the different aspects of your life; consider what's available to you in the way of technology and information. Everything is a potential resource. Your list may not be long, but it will be a way for you to leverage what you already have.

I'm an advocate of simplification and shortcuts. If you can find a faster way of getting something done, do it. One of your strategies might be to accomplish something you don't know how to do, and one of your tactics might be to learn it. However, another approach might be to hire somebody or find a partner who already has that knowledge. By getting clear about your resources, you can cross-reference them with your dreams and projects, and determine how things might come together.

Strategies and steps do go hand in hand. When you have developed your list of strategies and steps, code them in a way that tells you at a glance what you have to do to accomplish them:

S All you have to do is *schedule* this item.

B This strategy or step is a way for you to *be,* rather than something you have to do.

P This strategy or step needs a *plan* to develop it further so that it can be scheduled into your calendar.

D This is my favorite letter, because it means *"done."* It's wonderful when you can see what you've accomplished and that you're moving forward on your project.

STRATEGIES AND STEPS:
A ROAD MAP FOR GETTING THERE

STRATEGIES: Your Approach to Achieving Your Dream

1. _____

2. _____

3. _____

4. _____

5. _____

STEPS: Your "To Do" List
(Complete for each of the strategies you list above.)

Date	Item	Resource
____	_____	_____
____	_____	_____
____	_____	_____
____	_____	_____
____	_____	_____
____	_____	_____
____	_____	_____

SCHEDULING

Put the items "to do" in chronological order and transfer them to your calendar.

Month _____

Day _____   To do _____

_____   _____

_____   _____

_____   _____

_____   _____

Month _____

Day _____   To do _____

_____   _____

_____   _____

_____   _____

_____   _____

Month _____

Day _____   To do _____

_____   _____

_____   _____

_____   _____

_____   _____

When you get to this stage, it's important to differentiate between a project and a specific step. It's a lot easier to get into action on a single step than it is on a whole project. You know that old joke, "How do you eat an elephant?" "A bite at a time." That's how you will accomplish your project, one manageable bite at a time.

MY RESOURCES

People and Organizations Who Can Help Me

Friends who can help me: _____

_____

Friends of friends who can help me: _____

_____

Family members who can help me: _____

_____

Business associates who can help me: _____

_____

Organizations or associations that can help me: _____

_____

Who will support me? _____

_____

Who can advise me? _____

_____

Who can really help me? _____

_____

People I don't know who can help me: _____

_____

Who is the one person who won't help me? _____

_____

How can I use even the person who won't help? _____

_____

Things I Can Do To Make My Dream Come True

Places I can go: _____

_____

Things I can read: _____

_____

New things I can try: _____

_____

Old things I can reference: _____

_____

The one place I know I can't get any help: _____

_____

How can I use this? _____

_____

THE DREAM BANK DEPOSIT SLIP

When you are looking for people who are committed to encouraging the possibilities in your life and to supporting your dreams, remember me. I'm one of those people. I believe that every aspect of all your dreams can come true, and I've created the Dream Bank, where you can deposit your dream with me.

I invite you to provide all the information requested on the Dream Bank deposit slip. Where it says, "My dream is ____," write out your dream and commit to an action step you will take within this next week. Get into action right away by creating a step and scheduling the date.

I recommend you create a "WOW," for "Within One Week." What action step will you take this week to move your dream forward? Make it simple and set yourself up for an easy win, a success.

Here are some of the dreams and WOW's that have been sent to me.

MY DREAM IS:

To have my pilot's license, and Within One Week, I completed my first solo flight.

To open a retreat center, and WOW (Within One Week), I began to scout international locations.

To invent and launch a new product. WOW I mapped out a strategy and had a team in place.

To be in a loving committed relationship. WOW I ran a personal ad and had two fun dates.

To have new fun experiences every day. WOW I renewed passion in my marriage.

To produce a nationally syndicated TV show. WOW I met with three cable stations.

To retire. WOW I mapped out a transition plan with my business partner.

To sing again (ex–Metropolitan Opera star). WOW I was singing again.

To triple my income. WOW I had my husband's support and a new team started.

To spend time reconnecting with my family. WOW I booked a family vacation.

DREAM BANK DEPOSIT SLIP

My dream is _____

_____

_____

My WOW (within one week) is _____

Name: _____

Address: _____

_____

Phone: (Home) _____ (Office) _____

E-mail: _____

When you have completed your deposit slip, photocopy the page, and send it to me by mail, fax, or e-mail. My contact information is in the back of this book. When I receive your deposit slip, you'll become part of a global network, a DreamTeam for people all over the world with all kinds of dreams.

If you choose not to send it to my Dream Bank, fill in the deposit slip and tape it to your mirror, or put it in some other place where you'll read it daily. It's powerful, however, to have your dreams registered with someone who believes they can come true. I'll be that person for you; I believe in you and in your having what you want.

Is it both exciting and confronting to commit to an action step? Of course, and hopefully it will be a positive and important step. Read about Judy and how when she filled out her Dream Bank deposit slip, she became angry. All kinds of limiting beliefs came up. But committing to an action item and taking that first step was a life-changing experience for her.

Real People: JUDY

Judy was a talented singer and performer, but she decided early in her career to postpone her music dreams and marry a wonderful man. Although she sang in the church choir, her main goal in life was to be a great wife and mom. Her family and home were her first priority. She was grateful that she could provide marketing services for Tony Orlando in the town of Branson, Missouri, where she lived. But as she went through this dream process, there was no denying that she was a singer at heart, although that was a well-kept secret, especially from Tony.

On her Dream Bank deposit slip, her WOW commitment was that at age forty-four, she would set up an audition with her friend Norman Berger, a music producer who sang with the Tokens and who had arranged the original version of "The Lion Sleeps Tonight."

Immediately Judy got upset because she didn't see how her dream of singing professionally could happen. Judy's life had been dedicated to others and the thought of pursuing her own dream felt overwhelming, frustrating, and even impossible. Casey, her daughter, asked her what was going on, and with great insight this eighteen-year-old said, "Mom, I'm grown up. I release you to pursue your dreams." It's no wonder why Casey went on to win Miss American Teen shortly after this. She continues to be a great DreamTeam member for her mom.

Judy's life changed, but it started by her writing her dream and action step and then sharing it. Within a week she called Norman. They went into a studio, and halfway through the first song, he turned to the technician and said, "She needs to do a CD." On her wedding anniversary that year, her husband Rob took her into the studio and with some of the members of Tony Orlando's band she recorded "May the Circle Be Unbroken." What a great DreamTeam song. And shortly after that, Judy sold several original country songs to up-and-coming artists.

There was one more element of her dream. Judy showed up many nights in the audience of Tony's shows. Since she had worked for him, he was always glad to see her, but had no idea that she had this amazing gift and talent.

Most nights, he would walk out into the audience and hand the microphone to various people, inviting them to sing a bit. When Judy motioned for him to give her the mike, he was surprised and a little confused, but only for a moment. Her singing stopped him in his tracks. She later told him she had a dream and wanted his help. She made a very specific request: "I want to be in your show. Can I?" On the opening night of his Christmas show, "Santa and Me," Tony said to Judy, "You—every show, starting tomorrow."

Register your dreams

with someone who believes

that they can come true.

Real People: BRIAN

Brian, who wanted to start a new company, needed to find office space. The steps he took were (1) to look at a certain number of spaces by a specific date; (2) to review his resources; (3) to speak with owners of other companies about sharing space; and (4) to be in a new office within a certain time frame. The most powerful step of all was that he committed himself to a specific date and wrote it on his calendar.

Brian also developed many other strategies: acquiring the necessary office equipment, producing marketing and promotional materials, setting up an accounting system, preparing a strategic plan for his board of directors, enlisting key people to support his vision, and raising funds. Financially, Brian's tactic was to break down his operating income: by a certain date he would know what his expenses would be, and he would then identify sources of funds. To simplify his pursuit he broke down even those specifics into additional strategies and steps. By breaking all his strategies down into specific steps to take, Brian successfully accomplished his project and his dream, one step at a time.

It's a lot easier

to get into action on one step

than it is on a whole project,

and one step moves you

forward on your dream.

CHAPTER 12

Playing on a Winning DreamTeam

**A burning purpose attracts others
who are drawn along with it and help fulfill it.**

—MARGARET BOURKE-WHITE

SOME PEOPLE STILL HARBOR the old belief that they have to do everything themselves. Perhaps it's that old John Wayne–type, individualistic American frontier attitude. If you feel that standing on your own two feet means never accepting help from anyone, it's important to acknowledge the tendency. Of course, you *can* go it alone if you insist, but it's a longer, harder process.

I caution you, however, not to take on everything by yourself. You want to simplify the journey to having your dream, not complicate it. If you're part of a winning team, you can accelerate progress and expand your horizons. In short, it's easier and faster to accomplish things with help from other people.

When I speak of a winning DreamTeam, I don't necessarily mean a club or a group that meets with regularity. Formal groups have potential for some people and not for others. Rather, I think of a winning team as a resource group, people to whom you can turn when you need advice, when you need a sounding board, when you need to solve a thorny problem, or when you need someone to listen.

Although we all tend not to want to bother others or to recruit assistance, what happens when two or more are gathered is uncanny. I personally believe you're only a few phone calls away from anyone in the world that you need to contact. Use this to your advantage.

You want to simplify the journey to having your dream, not complicate it.

Letting others help you is a form of generosity, because you enable them to feel good about contributing to your success. Many people love to make a difference by helping others. You can allow people to assist you most effectively by learning how to make powerful requests. Get clear about what you need, find the individuals who can help you get it, and ask for what you want.

One of the tools you can use to decide what skills you need on your team is to develop written criteria. On page 151, list your requirements for the members of your winning team.

ENROLLING OTHERS: YOUR CURRENT RESOURCES

There are many reasons why others will be interested in helping you. After all, you're a go-getter with a big dream; in its completion, your dream might benefit others. What happens as a result of enrollment is beyond anything you can imagine. Invite people to be on your DreamTeam. Here's a tip: make specific requests, as Judy did with Tony Orlando, so that it will be easy for people to say yes.

For example, one of my dreams was to be out in the world speaking about something in which I believed. I shared my dream and connected, through a friend of a friend, with the director of creative services for a national television network. That person eventually scheduled me on a nationwide talk show, something that never would have happened if I had not spoken about my dream.

With whom should you speak? Begin by reviewing the Resources forms you completed in Chapter 11, to see who's currently available to help you. Start talking to those people about your dream. Tell them what it is you're committed to; help them to experience your excitement by sharing your enthusiasm with them.

Then ask your resources who else they know. Remember, you're only one phone call away from somebody you need to reach, two at the most. By asking those you know to name others, you are developing a network. Before long you will have clarified your needs and you'll start to understand who you want on your team. Find at least one person who believes in your dream, and sometimes the more the merrier.

You know some people right now who can fill spots on your team immediately, and you'll find others during the process. If you need a confidant, someone to whom you can tell all your secrets, look around among your resources; that person may already exist. If you have no one with business savvy among your current resources, find out if anyone you know is acquainted with such a person; if not, go out and find the individuals with the skills you need.

CRITERIA FOR MEMBERS OF YOUR DREAMTEAM

Skills: _____

_____

_____

Interests: _____

_____

_____

Education: _____

_____

_____

Resources: _____

_____

_____

Other: _____

_____

_____

_____

_____

The people you need

to help you make your dream come true

are everywhere, and within your reach.

ENROLLING OTHERS: NEW RESOURCES

Your team need not be composed only of people who are currently on your list of resources. When you need additional skills on the team, add members who are outside of your immediate universe.

You can find new people with the skills you need by identifying groups and associations to which they may belong. Several directories list organizations by subject area—*Gale's Encyclopedia of Associations,* for example, and the *National Trade and Professional Associations of the United States.* Ask people you already know what associations they belong to; look in the business section of your local newspaper to identify groups that meet in your area.

Plan to attend group meetings as a nonmember, go with your purpose in mind, and be clear about the desired result. Decide in advance what kind of people you want to meet there, what you want to get out of the meeting, and what you want to communicate. Once you're there, you have an opportunity to develop relationships with all kinds of new people; plan to participate and interact with them. Always speak your dream.

Most people who attend such gatherings may shake a few hands, talk with one or two individuals, and then leave. You are not such a person, because you know the power of sharing your dream in a new group. You are now clear about your dream and can articulate it with clarity and passion. Talk about your dream the moment you walk into the room, and they will see you as a dynamic individual, committed to making your dream a reality.

You start with a blank slate among new people; capture the energy and input from those encounters. If you notice that someone is getting excited about your dream, ask how that individual would like to participate. Make it easy for the person to say yes.

Many ideas grow better when

transplanted into another mind,

than in the one where they sprang up.

—OLIVER WENDELL HOLMES JR.

It is also powerful to ask others about their commitment to their own dream. As they speak, you might discover a way to join with them and expand your vision. For instance, someone who's committed to literacy might be able to help you fulfill your dream of creating more jobs for people. Perhaps together you can find employment for previously unemployable people who have learned how to read. By listening to other people's dreams, you can hear about new possibilities, get new ideas, and find new resources.

Another way to enroll people onto your winning team is to become an active letter writer. Whenever someone who can further your dream is mentioned in a book or an article, or is featured on radio or television, note how to contact the publication or the station. Take a risk; write a letter, and tell that individual about your dream.

Perhaps you will be attending a convention featuring a speaker you'd like to have as part of your network. Write in advance and say how much you look forward to the presentation. While you're at the meeting, approach that person and introduce yourself; then write a quick follow-up letter when the meeting is over. These simple steps will take you little time and yield big results. By doing them, you will have made yourself part of that new person's consciousness and, in the months that follow, you can begin a dialogue in person.

Don't be afraid to call people on the phone. If you're not sure exactly what you want to say, write out a couple of points and keep them in front of you, or practice speaking to somebody else. You'll be amazed at how many well-known people answer their own phone and how accessible many of them are. Be prepared. Have a clear intention and be respectful of their time. Remember why you are calling them and make a specific request. My experience is that most people would like to say yes and be helpful, if they can.

Jeff Davidson, in his popular book *Blow Your Own Horn: How to Get Noticed—And Get Ahead,* suggests that you think about the ten people you need to call right now. Perhaps they include an association director, a magazine editor, or someone in another industry. You will find the task is less formidable if you break it down into its individual components. First, compile a list of the phone numbers and have them in front of you. Then commit to making a specific number of calls each day. Get into action.

Look for resources in your own company.
With whom can you speak about your dream when you go
    to work tomorrow morning?
Is your boss enrolled, or any of your co-workers?
Do they even know that you have a dream?

Have you already decided that they're not potential partners and they can't help you? Or are you sitting there thinking that you can't pursue your dream without your boss's support, even though your boss may not know what your dream is? Don't kill off possibilities before you've explored them.

Action makes more fortunes than caution.

—LUC DE CLAPIERS, MARQUIS DE VAUVENARGUES

Look for ways to share your dream and tie it into the other aspects of your life. It's essential that you enroll your family in your dream by communicating what you want. Let them hear your commitment and enthusiasm, and be unstoppable regardless of how they respond. Demonstrate your commitment by taking action. There really is no other way. As they see your commitment, no matter how big your dream may be, eventually they will stand behind you. Tenacity often results in credibility. Show them you're not giving up; ask them to support you, even if they can do so only by believing in you; and be open to accepting their support.

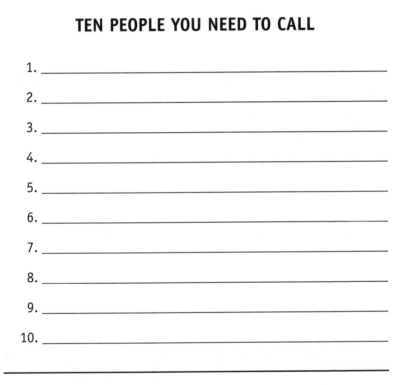

TEN PEOPLE YOU NEED TO CALL

1. _____

2. _____

3. _____

4. _____

5. _____

6. _____

7. _____

8. _____

9. _____

10. _____

Sometimes we feel absolutely sure that we will not get the support of the people from whom we most want it. Let them change their minds. Any day, any moment could be the moment they sign up to be on your team.

When you think about involving your family, notice your attitudes and beliefs. Is that voice inside your head saying, "My parents never thought I could do it" or "The family will think this is just another harebrained scheme"? Those are just your attitudes and beliefs; you can go back and write them in the Attitudes and Beliefs section in Chapter 6, but you don't have to include them in what you are designing for the future.

Be clear about what you're committed to, and start to speak it powerfully so that people around you can help. Get others on board, whether they play an intimate role in your dream or a tangential one. It's all part of building a winning team.

THE MEMBERS OF YOUR DREAMTEAM

One of the ways to engage others quickly is to make a request. Ask for something specific; the more precise the request, the more specific will be the response. Simply say, "I'd like to make a request of you." Your query can be accepted or rejected, or the other person can make a counteroffer. When you make a request, be willing to hear what people say in response.

Tenacity often results in credibility.

When you ask for something, you signal to others that your interest in what they have to offer is more than casual. They are likely to take you more seriously. You convey the message that you'd like to have an answer, that you're interested in moving the conversation, and possibly the relationship, forward.

Once you've got someone's attention, you can enlist his or her services in several ways. One of my favorite methods is to trade services. One woman I know conducts public relations activities for her certified public accountant in exchange for accounting assistance. Someone else trades strategic planning services for massage therapy; another barters coaching for cooking.

If you think you don't have anything to barter, reexamine what you're passionate about. Most of us can offer some kind of service in exchange for another. It's a great way of experiencing what you're capable of doing.

THE SKILLS ON YOUR TEAM

You will need many different skills on your winning team, although you can expect your needs to change over time. As you develop new projects and complete old ones, you may find your-self in need of skills you did not consider important earlier. There are, however, three kinds of people you will always need on your team: mentors, coaches, and partners.

Mentors: People who know the ropes are an invaluable asset. The skills required of a mentor are perhaps the easiest to define and the easiest to find. If you are looking for someone who can teach you how to move forward quickly, how to create shortcuts, or how to break into a new area, you need only seek someone with expertise in the field. An experienced lawyer, for example, can mentor a young attorney. A woman who runs her own estab-lished business can guide an entrepreneur who is just starting out. An experienced writer can assist a fledgling author. Look for someone who has been where you want to go, is still learning and growing, and is happy to share those experiences with you.

Mentors: _____

_____

_____

_____

Coaches: _____

_____

_____

_____

Partners: _____

_____

_____

_____

Coaches: A coach is someone who listens for what's possible, helps you break through when you're stuck, and holds you accountable for doing what you said you were going to do. The coaching concept has really caught on, and trained professionals are now available for hire, some perhaps right in your backyard. Check out the Association of Personal and Professional Coaches.

You can employ a strategic planner or a marketing specialist, or you can train a close friend to take your dreams seriously and support you in your efforts. You can be there for each other. Look for someone with qualities you admire: strength of character, clarity of vision, commitment, dependability. Once you identify your coach, design the coaching relationship using some or all of the following questions:

In what area do you want to be coached?
What specific, measurable result do you want to achieve?
What is your weekly campaign of activities?
How often will you and your coach speak and for how long?
How do you want to be coached?
Do you want to know what you're doing right and wrong?
Will you hear criticism as coaching, or will you hear it as judgment?

Partners: Partners will give, receive, and share equally with you as members of your winning team. You can develop partnerships with individuals who are already in your life—family members, friends, business associates—or with organizations and groups of individuals. When you know what result you want from a partner, seek out candidates. Simply picking up the phone and having a conversation with someone might initiate something new. A project is the glue that will allow you and your partner to work together. Design a venture you're both clear about, with specific, measurable results; out of that, the partnership will develop.

As you review your list of resources, you might notice that there are dozens of people in your life of whom you never thought to make a request. You may also find unique combinations of individuals whom you never before thought of putting together.

You won't want to feel overwhelmed, however, about where you'll find the time for new ventures. If you're creating your winning team on track, everything you do will support your purpose, enhance your dreams, and be filled with passion. That's always your touchstone for making sure that you're on target toward making your dream come true.

I rarely come across a dream or project that wouldn't benefit from a team. I'm also often asked by skeptics, "Can you really design a strategy for any dream, even finding a new relationship?" Read about Gwen and the team she assembled around her dream to meet a man. My shortcut strategy for meeting new relationship candidates is to flirt. By that I mean be friendly. Experience shows that we all wait for the other person to initiate conversation. I once made an overture to a very powerful and successful man. As our relationship flourished, he told me that we would have never gotten together had I not made the first move. Although he is comfortable talking to thousands of people, heads of state, and presidents, he feels awkward starting a conversation with a woman. Unbelievable, perhaps, yet true.

Real People: GWEN

Gwen's professional life was sailing along, but by the time she hit her late thirties a new dream was taking precedence. She wanted to be in a loving relationship with her dream man and have a family. She realized that for this to happen she needed to share her dream and recruit a solid DreamTeam to help her.

She went online and sent out the following e-mail message to twenty friends and associates. It said, I am sending you this note with three specific requests:

1. Will you be on my DreamTeam? Yes means you will hold my dream in your heart and check in with me to see that I am taking action on my dream.
2. Please read my vision of the kind of relationship that I am seeking and the qualities that I desire in a man.

3. Please introduce me to any and all eligible bachelors that you believe are potential candidates for a match with me. I trust you.

Her e-mail letter went on to include her wish list and closed by saying, "The more I voice who I am, what I am seeking, and what I love, the sooner I will have what my heart desires." Her friends responded very supportively—always the sign of true friends. They told her they thought this was a bold move and they would help her. Gwen has been having lots of dates and continues to share her dream. I just called her for an update, and she said there is now a new man in her life.

You too can assemble a DreamTeam to help you achieve your dream. Use your resources—and remember that the Internet can be the ultimate dream machine.

THE GOOSE STORY

Next fall when you see geese heading south for the winter, flying in V-formation, consider what science has discovered about why they fly that way:

As each bird flaps its wings, it creates
an uplift for the bird immediately following.
By flying in V-formation, the whole flock adds
at least seventy-one percent greater flying range than
if each bird flew on its own.
People who share a common direction
and sense of community

can get where they are going more quickly and easily
because they are traveling on the thrust of one another.
When a goose falls out of formation,
it suddenly feels the drag
and resistance of trying to go it alone . . .
and quickly gets back into
formation to take advantage of the lifting power
of the bird in front.
If we have as much sense as a goose we will stay in
formation with those who are headed the same way we are.
When the head goose gets tired, it rotates back
in the wing and another goose flies point.
It is sensible to take turns doing demanding jobs
with people or with geese flying south.
Geese honk from behind to encourage those up
front to keep up their speed.
What do we say when we honk from behind?
Finally—and this is important—
when a goose gets sick or is wounded by gunshots and
falls out of formation,
two other geese fall out with that goose
and follow it down to provide help and protection.
They stay with the fallen goose until it is able to fly,
or until it dies; only then do they set out on their own
or with another formation to catch up with their group.
If we have the sense of a goose,
we will stand by each other like that.

—SOURCE UNKNOWN

CHAPTER 13

Communicating Your Dream as a Way of Living

The difference between the right word and the almost right word is the difference between lightning and the lightning bug.

—MARK TWAIN

YOU HAVE ASSEMBLED A WINNING TEAM, and you've become adept at attracting more and more people who are interested in what you're doing. To accelerate toward your dream, you will want to continue communicating successfully with your team and with others as well.

The members of your team need to hear you speak about your dream, so they will know how they can help you. You might feel a little awkward at first, but the more you articulate your dream, the more powerful you'll become. Like anything else, this requires practice. In today's world, people are inundated by enormous amounts of information competing for their attention. In 1968, for example, the portion of a statement or speech used for television news, called a sound bite, ran an average of forty-two seconds. By 1988, sound bites were down to 9.8 seconds. And with the addition of the Internet, we enter the twenty-first century in information overload.

In other words, you have less than ten seconds to speak your dream; that's about how much time you have for someone to understand what you're trying to do. If you want to break through the information din, practice saying what you want to say, and see if you can get it across clearly and comfortably in ten seconds.

This ten-second exercise may surprise you. You can complete three sentences in that short time. For example, the words you are reading in this paragraph can be spoken in about ten seconds.

On page 166 you're asked to write your dream or your project in twenty-five words or less. Write it, practice speaking it aloud, and then practice by speaking it to other people. If others don't understand your message immediately, revise it until they do. Here are some examples of brief, clear descriptions:

> ➤ I intend to contact and speak with one hundred people about preservation of the rain forest, and to create a television series about it.
> ➤ I'm going to hold a one-day seminar for children of divorced parents.
> ➤ I will make available to all employees in the Washington, D.C., area an effective program for retirement savings.
> ➤ I plan to create the best possible relationship with a man.
> ➤ I will make my department the most successful in the company.

The expression of what you want can be simple or sophisticated. Base your decision on the nature of the dream you're committed to creating. Mine is to have people speak about dreams in a new way, to believe that dreams are something they can have come true in their lifetime. What's yours?

_____

An orator is a man who says

what he thinks and feels what he says.

—WILLIAM JENNINGS BRYAN

_____

COMMUNICATING YOUR DREAM

In 25 words or less, write in the space below a clear description of your dream or your project.

_____

_____

_____

_____

_____

_____

_____

Now rate yourself on the Passion Scale. If you're not excited about your dream, others won't be either. Listen to yourself; hear how you sound. See how you feel. Tell us about your dream.

PASSION SCALE

Place an X next to the term that best describes your level of passion regarding speaking about your dream or project. Do it right now.

_____ Red hot
_____ Turned on
_____ Excited
_____ Very interested
_____ Interested
_____ Some possibility
_____ No interest

WHO'S LISTENING?

When you tell people what your dream is, you will want to know whether they've heard you. Look into their eyes. Do they look confused or upset about what you're saying or are they excited and "with you"? Do they understand? If you're not sure, stop and find out. Ask them what they think. If they're not excited about your dream, it doesn't mean that you did something wrong; it may not be the right dream for them. Perhaps they can still be your friends or business associates, but they're not people you want on your team.

Notice who's listening and how they're listening, and invite them to hear what you're saying in a way that's powerful. Remember that when *you* started to go for your dream, you had certain negative attitudes, beliefs, concerns, and fears; others might also harbor attitudes that are limiting. People who care about you may feel especially convinced that you're going in the wrong direction, taking too much risk, or putting yourself in an unstable situation by breaking out of the norm.

Train people to listen to you. Explain what the word "possibility" means, and ask them to hear what's possible for *you*. Request that they suspend their automatic negative reactions and judgments and hear your dream from your perspective.

You don't necessarily have to convince people to see things your way to receive their support. It may take them a while before they're comfortable about accepting your dream. In the meantime, commit yourself to the possibility of getting their support in exactly the way you've asked for it. Believe that you can have that kind of a relationship, and keep speaking about your dream.

Notice who's listening to you

and how they're listening,

and invite them to hear what you're saying

in a way that's powerful.

You may not want to speak all of your dream in one sitting if you think it will overwhelm people. You can do it in stages; keep living and speaking what you want, and share it with others so they can understand what's going on for you. Eventually they will reach the stage at which, whether times are good or bad, you can share your dream completely.

Maybe everyone won't reach that stage. At some point you may decide that a particular person won't fit on your Dream-Team. That happens sometimes, and it's good to know when you have enough information to make that decision. However, I encourage you not to write people off at the beginning if they don't align with your dream. Request that they react as you would like, and give them a chance to do so.

I know there are schools of thought that say you should not indiscriminately share your dreams and I respect that. But if you are not sharing your dreams with many people, you may be missing some wonderful and unexpected opportunities for help. Then of course there are those negative people, the dream stealers and dream killers, to be aware of. One woman told me that her own mother is so negative that she stopped sharing her dreams with her. Then one day she had this insight: "If everything in life serves a function, I wonder what my mother's negative attitude could serve?" She got it. Whenever she is ready to launch a new product or service, she calls her mother. As expected, her mom tells her everything that could possibly go wrong. The daughter then designs strategies to manage all those potential obstacles. She overcame her limiting belief about her mother's negativity and found a way to use and benefit from it.

When you share your dream, it's okay also to speak about your fears and concerns. If others are facing the same fears and concerns, the issues can be put on the table for discussion. You may recall that we spoke earlier of the importance of honesty about your current reality; sharing that truth with another person can be an insightful experience.

Part of the communication process involves the dance of inter-action. Trust, let the conversation flow, and listen to what is being said. Something new might come up: perhaps others know of a new resource; maybe they will suggest a new way for you to look at something. Don't be rigidly attached to what is already in your mind. In speaking your dream, new opportunities will show up. Keep your eyes and ears open. Expect success.

The story of Gillian, on page 171, illustrates the benefits of enrolling others. What's important about Gillian's tale is that a major international event started with somebody's dream. The vision became bigger and took on new form when Gillian began speaking her dream and enrolling others. All kinds of opportunities showed up, and different people became part of the winning team and worked to make it a success.

This is an example of how a dream became a reality, how communication and sharing got people enrolled and excited, and how the dream became bigger and better than what any individual at first thought was possible.

Don't write people off automatically if,

at the beginning, they don't

align with your dream.

Request that they react as you would like,

and give them a chance to do so.

Real People: GILLIAN

Gillian was the head of the U.S. contingent of the World Association of Women Entrepreneurs. Her dream was to invite women from all over the world to Washington, D.C., where they would be treated in a special way.

Gillian spoke her dream to me and I became excited about it. Together we organized a group of women to brainstorm around her idea. I came up with the dream. We would hold a major luncheon and international media event at the National Press Club in the nation's capital.

When you begin speaking your dream

and enrolling others,

your dream can get bigger

and take on new forms,

and all kinds of

opportunities will show up.

The objective of this event was to honor women entrepreneurs from thirty countries around the world and to have them recognized by other women business owners, corporations, government officials, and the media. The exposure and visibility were expected to garner greater national attention and additional funds for the organization, increase the U.S. membership, and boost the organization's international membership.

As the brainstorming continued, we decided to create a Declaration of International Partnership. We developed a document that focused on five areas in which women business owners could make an impact: education, environment, enterprise, communication, and innovation. Some five hundred people attended the sellout event and you could hear a pin drop as each of the thirty country presidents signed the document. It was hailed as a historic event and got major TV and print exposure, including coverage in the international edition of *USA Today*. And just for the record, no budget was available for producing this stellar event. Funds were raised and corporate sponsors signed on because it was an amazing vision expressed with great passion. Every dream starts with an idea and grows proportionately to the amount of energy, excitement, and commitment behind it.

CHAPTER 14

Designing Your Environment

Two stonecutters were asked what they were doing. The first said, "I'm cutting this stone into blocks." The second replied, "I'm on a team that's building a cathedral."

—OLD STORY

ENROLLING OTHERS TO SUPPORT your dream is one important aspect of using resources. Another is designing your environment. As you progress on the path to making your dream come true, and you begin to realize that more and more is possible, additional opportunities and resources begin to become available. Whereas you may once have been concerned about not having any real possibilities, now you may feel overwhelmed by them.

The process is dynamic and ongoing. As you enroll people in your dream, you generate additional projects. As you take on other projects and develop new resources, you discover other people you wish to enroll. The new people lead you to new projects, and you find yourself constantly rearranging your physical and emotional environment to support your new endeavors.

The point of designing your environment is to create an atmosphere that will accommodate your changing needs while remaining clutter-free. You began the process way back in Chapter 1, when you first started looking at your dream. That is, after all, the environment for which you are designing. Aligning your dreams with your purpose—removing the inconsistencies— was just another way of removing clutter.

As you progress on the path

to making your dream come true,

you begin to realize

that more and more is possible.

You might start this phase of designing your environment with something as simple as cleaning off your desk or organizing a special room. At the end of this chapter you'll read more about Judy, the singer whose story you heard in Chapter 11, and how she made her dream real by setting up a space that would literally support her.

Many books have been written about eliminating physical clutter. Don't belabor it; *do* it so you will have space to continue creating and reaching for your dream. Similarly, if emotional issues are keeping you from being clear about what your dream will look like, or about how you'll find the time to get it, clear them out of your way.

FINDING TIME

Time is a funny thing. Sometimes we feel that it's closing in around us; but when there's something we're passionate about, we create a way to make it happen. I wrote my book *Doing Less and Having More* primarily because I so often heard people say, "Not only do I not have time to make my dreams happen, I don't even have time to know what my dreams are." So I wrote a book that teaches you how to make your life easier so you will have more time and greater ease.

Each of my project files has a list of strategies and steps—"to do" items—attached to the front of it. If I'm in my office with an extra hour between calls, I can pull out one of my project files, do any item on the list, and I'm in action on something I love. My projects are the mechanisms for fulfilling my life's purpose. I spend most of my time working on my projects. At the end of the day or the week, when I want to plan ahead, I look at my project files and create the next week. This is the process—known as living by design—for actually creating a dream-come-true life. Learn to live more from your passion and less from your calendar or, better yet, fill your calendar with the steps for achieving your dreams.

It takes focus and commitment to design your whole life to work this way. It takes time, too, to learn a completely new way to live, think, and plan. Here's a little incentive: I have often seen people with passion and intention go farther in life and on their dreams than those who have only skill and experience.

As you prepare to redesign your life, keep it simple at first, so you won't feel overwhelmed. Perhaps there's one area in which you can start to live on purpose, one dream that matters to you, one project that will ignite the passion in you. Maybe it's a project that does not exist yet. Maybe it's something you're going to create that comes from your heart. If you schedule it, and if it matters to you, I promise that you'll find the time to do it.

Even if you are employed by a company where most of the projects you work on are assigned by someone else, you can still find one area where you're in control. Then you can slowly begin to work on other areas. Maybe there's a project you can bring into your company, or perhaps a project already exists to which you're not now assigned but which is in alignment with your interests. If you're not passionate at work, think about what quality you can bring to your job that will allow you to express more passion there. Maybe there's a piece of something you feel passionate about that you can integrate into a work project—your love of learning, perhaps, or a desire to help others or to be creative. One man I know has a passion for baseball. He turned a tedious task into a friendly yet competitive game. He divided his colleagues into two teams, donned an umpire's uniform, and yelled, "Play ball." Which they did. They accomplished a huge warehouse inventory in record time, and they all went out for beer afterward to celebrate.

Projects are the mechanism for fulfilling your life's purpose.

If you can't invest your job with passion, perhaps you are turned on by an issue in your community. Follow your passion. Pursue what has heart and meaning for you.

SIMPLIFY

If you have so many things going on in your life that you need to clear some out before you can get to higher ground, then you need to simplify. Here's how.

Go back to your purpose, the simple, broad terms of who you are, and revisit your dreams. Cross-reference that massive list of "to do" items, projects, and all the other things you've got going on, and see how they align with your dreams. Perhaps amid all that clutter there's actually something missing, an area left out of your dreams, such as having a balanced life.

Now you have another choice to make. You can add another dream, or you can take a critical look at your projects to see if you're committed to all of them. Perhaps they're not all on your A-list. If you're compulsive about not giving anything up and you feel that you're committed to everything, then maybe there's something you don't absolutely have to do this year. Or you may decide that it's fine to eliminate the four or five projects you feel burdened by, the ones that aren't even listed under a dream you think is important. Or you could get some help.

There is always a way to create

a life that supports who you are,

and there are always places

where things can be relaxed.

You can ease up in your desire to have something, your commitment to it, your schedule, or the degree to which you need it. It all starts with that foundation called your life's purpose, the "Who are you, really?" and "Just what are you committed to?"

There are other ways to design your environment besides clearing out the clutter and finding time. I like to create a blueprint, a mechanism for getting from point A to point B. In the Real People story at the end of this chapter, you will see we created a symbol for David, using simple imagery that will keep his commitment (literally) at hand.

Perhaps all you need to begin designing your own environment is to cut out photos from a magazine and hang them in a prominent place. Some people like to create a dream board or collage, so they can keep visual images of what they want right in front of them. Maybe, like David, there's something you can develop as part of your physical self so that you can stay easily in touch with our dream and always keep it near by.

SHORTCUTS AND THE MYTH OF PREREQUISITES

With his five professional areas mapped out and in front of him, David started looking for shortcuts to his dream and for short-circuits in his beliefs. His search for short-circuits was appropriate; that small voice in his head was telling him that he had to do A before he could do B. Everyone has such internal dialogues: I'll do it when I have the money, when I get the education, when my family's ready to support me, after my children are grown.

A woman once told me that she always wanted to be a doctor, but she never could amass the time or money to go to medical school.

When she got in touch with what made her feel passionate, she saw that she wanted to work in the medical field, but she didn't want to be a doctor. When she was relieved of the burdens of figuring out how she would go through medical school, she quickly arranged for the training she needed to become an emergency medical technician.

Tie things together

to simplify the journey

on the road to your dream.

Sometimes people become paralyzed by the belief that, to move on, they need certain additional skills or assets. Yet often resources are readily available to help them move quickly through the process of getting their dream. One method, of course, is to develop new skills; another is to hire somebody with the skills to do it for you. Following the advice of mentors, coaches, and partners is another great way to find a shortcut.

In addition to external resources, you have, in yourself, a major resource. You can move yourself forward by being clear about what you want to do, by deciding whether your goals in one area support those in another, and by tying things together to simplify the journey on the road to your dream.

If you're giving a speech, for example, and you tape it, you can use the tape to make other programs and to send to local radio stations. You could also try to market it or donate it to schools or libraries. You are in the best position to design your environment in ways to make your life easier. Make them up, try them on, and tie them together. Dream big.

One of your most powerful

inner resources

is your own creativity.

Be willing to try on

something new

and play the game full out.

One of your most powerful inner resources is your own creativity, your ability to imagine and interpret. Be willing to try on something new and play the game full out. Make requests of other people that are beyond what you thought was initially possible. Get up an hour earlier or an hour later. Flip through magazines you don't normally read. Find new ways to see things by trying on someone else's glasses, closing your eyes, and finding a new perspective, going to a children's movie or a play, relaxing, using your intuition. There are many methods of breaking out of your box; you need only to look for them, experiment, and try them on.

For example, there are many ways to look at your current life and the resources that you already have available. Have you considered, for example, all the places that you frequent in the course of a week?

Your office

Your health club

Your doctor's office

The supermarket

Movie theaters

Restaurants

Friends' homes

The park

Coffee shops

RESOURCES I HADN'T PREVIOUSLY CONSIDERED

_____

_____

_____

_____

_____

_____

_____

_____

_____

_____

_____

_____

_____

Perhaps there are resources among the people who supply you with goods or services. Maybe you can tap into something at your alma mater, through courses and seminars you've attended, or through teachers you've studied with. Think about all the cities in all the countries where you know people or have met people.

Everything in your life is a resource, especially yourself. Regard the way how *you* look and speak as a resource, not just the person with whom you are speaking. Are you friendly and open? Do you support the dreams of others? Are you studious? Do you have high powers of concentration? Do you go out dancing, to concerts, plays, or shows? Are you engaged with life?

What about the books you read, the videos you watch, the ideas you have, the energy you give off, even when you're dreaming in your sleep at night? Everything that you experience is a resource you can use to design your environment. How are you using your resources?

You don't have to go somewhere

in order to be free;

you can be free anywhere.

FREEDOM—LETTING GO

Many of us have a very basic dream that has to do with freedom. I'd love to have the freedom to do whatever I want whenever I want, the freedom to travel anywhere and everywhere, and—my favorite—the freedom to shop without worrying about the cost.

However, many of us are stuck with that old belief about prerequisites—the idea that we have to do something or have something in order to be free. For a long time I wanted to move to

California. I decided I'd move as soon as I could sell my Washington, D.C., condominium. Months went by and it didn't sell. I knew that there was something for me to learn in this.

One day I pulled out my journal and asked myself, "What will I do or be in California that I'm not doing or being here and now in Washington, D.C.?" What a splendid question!

On my "doing" list I wrote, "playing tennis, doing lunch, growing my hair long, shortening my skirts, dancing, not working every day, public speaking." On my "being" list I wrote, "playing, relaxing, listening, waking without an alarm clock, breathing, believing, and being near the water."

I began to do and be everything on my lists while I was still in D.C., and everything I wanted, to my surprise and delight, was available. That brought me to a major revelation: I could be free anywhere. I didn't have to go somewhere or do something in order to be free.

Once I had arrived at that realization, it was easy for me to let go of an old belief that was keeping me from the freedom I wanted, and I sold the condo. As a matter of fact, I committed to moving west before the sale, and then the sale happened.

MONEY MADNESS

The lack of money is probably the most overworked excuse for not having what we want and for not pursuing our dreams. We say, "If I only had a million dollars, I'd go for my dream."

My response to this is "Do it anyway. Find a way to be in action. Develop alternatives. Get creative. Don't let a lack of money stop you. Find or devise the means to start now." Before I was able to sell my condo, I rented it out, and if I hadn't rented it, I would have found another way. As Joseph Kennedy Sr. said, "When the going gets tough, the tough get going."

Find yourself a different perspective. Trust me—money doesn't need to be the obstacle that keeps you from your dream. One couple I know is renting a magnificent multimillion dollar home, paying less than two thousand dollars a month. Here's how they did it.

Are you holding on

to the very thing

you want to be free of?

They saw and fell in love with a house that had been for sale and on the market for a long time. They contacted the owners and passionately described how if they lived in this home they would take great care of it. They described their dream and said that as landscapers, they would make this home even more beautiful, especially the gardens. The owner got excited about the idea, and this couple has happily been renting this mansion for almost a year. Money did not have to be what stopped them from having what they wanted, even though this dream appeared to be beyond their means.

Figure out your belief about money, and then determine your attitude toward money and toward your dreams. Find another way in. Use money as a motivator or as a stepping-stone, a bridge from where you are to where you want to be.

If you hear yourself using a lack of money as an excuse, don't you believe it. There's something else going on. Check your core beliefs, change your core beliefs using the information in Chapter 7, and do what you love. The money will follow. Of course, money *is* one way to gain freedom, but it's not the only way. Dr. Martin Luther King Jr. once said that if he were locked up in prison he would still be free, because freedom lived in his heart. Now, that's freedom!

What prerequisites have you put in your own way that slow you down or keep you from having your dream? Are they real? Are they necessary? Is there another way to move forward?

Real People: JUDY

Judy was committed to setting up all of her music paraphernalia and creating a space where she could write and sing. She reminded herself that she was already a singer by pulling out autographed photos of some of the people she had worked with years ago including the Platters and Jim Stafford. This process of gathering her mementos and displaying them was a powerful step for Judy.

These images became a daily reminder of the memories that she loved and of her current dream. When she moved her keyboard into the room and put up a huge music banner, her office was instantly transformed into an environment that expressed her passion. It was now her music room, the place where she would pursue her dream. It was from here that she made the phone call to her colleague that led to her recording session. And it took her only one day to create this space in her home.

Real People: DAVID

David is a television and film director who wanted to do some quick blueprinting of the design for his life. We were having dinner at a restaurant in Los Angeles. The restaurant used paper tablecloths and made crayons available for patrons to amuse themselves while they waited for their food. David and I got into a conversation about what made him feel passionate, then we picked up some crayons and started to design David's environment. It was evident that David's purpose was to be creative.

He said that he was turned on by five areas of his professional life: producing, directing, editing, acting, and writing. We brainstormed to find a symbol that he could always keep with him to remind him of his five passionate dream areas. We decided to use the fingers on a hand. So we traced David's hand on the paper, wrote his name in his palm, and each one of his fingers became one of his five dreams. Imagine holding all your dreams in the palm of your hand. As soon as David felt this, he had another important realization. His success in life was also in his hands.

Coming from his purpose, David established one dream that he was committed to accomplishing in each area. Then he created three or four projects in every area, each project having specific results. David was excited about the process, and the whole year was extraordinary for him; everything he did professionally fit one of those five areas. Prior to doing the exercise, David felt he wasn't moving forward toward his dream. Now he had designed and organized it in a way that made him feel powerful and eager to get into action. Moreover, using his hand as a representation enabled David to reinforce with ease his dream and his commitment to it.

Imagine and explore.

Take a risk. Take a step.

CHAPTER 15

Trusting, Timing, and You

**I am not afraid of tomorrow,
for I have seen yesterday and I love today.**

—WILLIAM ALLEN WHITE

ON THE PATH TO MAKING YOUR DREAMS COME TRUE, you're going to meet up with an issue called trust. Trust is at the core of everything. It can allow your dream to come true or keep it from happening.

I don't know any other way to build self-trust than to make up a dream, put it out there in the world, give it all you've got, and then see where you wind up. Doing this repeatedly will not only help you trust yourself but will also build your self-confidence.

When you don't trust yourself, things get difficult, blocked, or stuck. They may even fall apart. You start to doubt—first your decision, then eventually everything. You may start to compromise on your dream and try to manipulate the situation. In your best attempt to control the outcome, you may unknowingly sabotage your own dream.

The key here is to notice what's going on. When you are aware of the doubts, fears, concerns, and second thoughts, you can stop for a moment and regain some clarity. Start by asking yourself, "What is so?" Better yet, write that question out, and write out what you're thinking or telling yourself about "What is so?" What stories are you making up that may be disempowering your dream? What are you not trusting and why? How can you move this obstacle, this mistrust or lack of trust out of your way? Get clear about what you don't trust and get to the bottom of it, the heart of the basic area in which you don't fully have faith in that can cost you your dream.

JUST

TRUST.

Practice letting it go by being more committed to your dream and creating empowering beliefs. Ask yourself what you can do to learn trust or to help you let go of your lack of trust.

Letting go will happen when you are clear about what you want, when you've done everything there is to do, and now you can relax. Stop controlling, holding back, fretting, and worrying. Just trust—two simpler words may never have been spoken; when it comes to your dream, there is nothing more profound.

Practice "just trust." It's a critical component for creating a life of joy and ease.

Do you trust yourself and others?
Do you trust your environment, the universe, the timing, and the process?

Do you trust that your dream will come true?

What actions are you taking to demonstrate that you do
trust?

Trust is a giant obstacle for many people. If you don't have
it, you'll have to find it, and you'll have to practice trusting
yourself above all. Trust the decisions you make, and believe
that you're entitled to want your dream and to realize it.
Trust comes first; that's what allows the extraordinary results to
show up.

An effective exercise is to list on a piece of paper the people
and things that you do trust and those that you don't. Dan, who
undertook this exercise, decided that he trusted himself, his wife,
his minister, one co-worker, one neighbor, his mother, and his
brother. He did not trust people outside his immediate environment, nor did he trust the natural process and timing of things.
He also didn't trust that he could have a dream bigger than what
already existed in his life. Writing this down brought it to the
front of his awareness. From here Dan could make conscious
choices to explore new options, perhaps to even practice being
more trusting.

Your reality can be much bigger

than your current capacity

for dreaming about it.

Notice what you trust and what you don't. What is based on facts and reality and what might be your limiting beliefs? Just because something hasn't been done before doesn't mean it can't be done now.

BEING BALANCED

One of the ways to develop trust in yourself and the things around you is to keep yourself healthy by being centered and balanced. Feeling good about yourself leads to greater self-confidence, which is one of the places that trust comes from. You are a product of what you eat, how you live, how you rest and recreate, and what you think. All of these things filter into how you feel about yourself and, ultimately, what you allow yourself to trust.

You can work at achieving balance by incorporating some relaxation exercises into your life. The secret is to act on your dream at your own pace, doing activities with which you feel comfortable. Take a few deep, cleansing breaths before you start a new task; closing your eyes and concentrating on your deep breathing will allow you to feel more centered. By being in the here and now you will be in touch with your life, and you will feel your passion all the time. This is not about designing a five-year plan for yourself and then spending another five years figuring out how to control your life and make it happen. It's not about having it all happen right now. It's giving yourself some flow and leeway about what you want, trusting the timing and the process, and being in action in some way each day on the things you love to do. It's really quite simple.

WHAT I WILL DO TODAY
TO MAKE A DIFFERENCE IN MY LIFE

Starting today, I will do the following for myself:

At home: _____

_____

_____

_____

At work: _____

_____

_____

_____

With others: _____

_____

_____

_____

Alone: _____

_____

_____

_____

The element that's critical to making the timing work in your life is to be present. To be here, right now, enjoying and living your life. Take a look at what matters to you that you're not doing, being, or having. What could you change or create right now that would make a difference? You don't have to restructure your entire life this minute; maybe breathing deeply is all you need right now. Sometimes it's a matter of life or breath. Are you too busy to breathe?

Use the space provided on page 192 to list the things you will start doing today. These can be simple things: taking an extra five minutes in the morning to stretch and relax, or spending thirty minutes at the end of the day reading the newspaper. Decide what you can do that will keep you centered and balanced.

IN THE FLOW

Being in the flow means that the timing of your life is working for you, that there's a level of synchronicity where things seem to happen. One of my clients spoke to me of his dream to be featured in the local newspaper. The next day he called to tell me that the paper, seemingly out of the blue, wanted to interview him.

Surprises happen when you're living in the flow; you can get in sync with the universe when you're not busy trying to control your life and manipulate everything. Slow down and relax, let go of some of your resistance, and things will seem to happen naturally.

Michelle decided that it was important for her business that she travel to Florida once a month, but she didn't know how she could work the expense into her budget. The next day a travel agency called to say that her name had been selected in a random drawing and that she'd won six round-trip tickets to Florida. Since then, the trips have proven so fruitful that she is considering relocating to Florida.

Yesterday I decided to hire a personal assistant. Last night, after I presented a workshop in San Francisco, a young woman came up to me and said, "If you ever need a personal assistant, I would be interested in working for you." I hadn't even announced it. She starts tomorrow.

Perhaps you have some beliefs about calls that seem to come out of the blue. Sometimes good things happen because we have paid our dues or because we are in the right place at the right time. Michelle's experience, winning the round-trip tickets, was pure synchronicity. She had done nothing to put herself on that particular path; it just happened. I was clear about what I wanted, and I believe things like this happen all the time. Maybe that's why they do.

This is by no means a trivial component of making your dream come true; letting go of your doubt and fear and being open to greater ease are critical parts of the process.

You can do other things to keep yourself centered and balanced. You can take walks in nature, go to the beach and listen to the ocean. Perhaps you will want to give yourself the gift of an extraordinary bath. Take it to the limit: light candles all over the bathroom, play soft music, pour beautiful oils into the tub, and place a bath pillow under your head. Relax, calm yourself, and retreat from worldly concerns. I know city people who sit close to fountains and listen to the splashing water. For many this is the perfect time and place to dream on a whole different level.

WHEN LIFE HANDS YOU MORE AND MORE

When life brings you wonderful surprises, as it inevitably will, you might begin to be concerned that you'll have too many things coming at you too fast. After all, if you enroll people in your dream, others will start trying to enroll you in theirs. As more and more possibilities become evident, how will you know when to say yes and when to say no?

The possibilities are unlimited

as long as you are

true to your life's purpose.

Here are some simple questions you can ask yourself to determine whether or not this is right for you:

- ➤ Is this what I want to do now?
- ➤ Is this part of my dream?
- ➤ Is this something I'm passionate or excited about?

You'll know the right answer; it generally comes automatically. You'll know when you're excited about something, or when it seems like a duty. Don't be afraid to affix labels: "This is something I feel obligated to do." If that's the way you feel, you might let that project go. Other, more passion-provoking opportunities are available. In fact, the possibilities are unlimited as long as you honor yourself. Follow what has heart and meaning for you. Be willing to say yes; be willing to say, "I'll think about it," and be willing to say, "No, thank you." This is an essential skill to cultivate.

CHAPTER 16

Dare to Dream Big

**Never doubt that a small group of thoughtful,
committed citizens can change the world;
indeed it's the only thing that ever has.**

—MARGARET MEAD

SO FAR WE'VE FOCUSED on you and your dream; now we're
going to turn a corner. The goal of this chapter is to inspire you
to dream bigger—to go beyond what you've chosen so far.

If you want to have a life that's filled with passion, I encourage you to create a project that's bigger than your life. This project is a big one, perhaps one that you don't know how to accomplish, but one that comes from your passion.

Once you're clear about what you're committed to, incredible resources, possibilities, and people will show up to help you. Although it may not be completed during your lifetime, it will allow you to play an extraordinary game. You will definitely feel passion.

Imagine dreaming of a loving world that works, or of creating heaven on earth in your own special way. Many big dreamers came before you—Kennedy, King, Gandhi—but everyday people absolutely can make a contribution to the world. Pursuing your big dream is not only about doing what you say or what you want; it means actually being and becoming a different kind of person.

I have not the shadow of a doubt that

any man or woman can achieve what I have,

if he or she would make the same effort

and cultivate the same hope and faith.

What is faith if it is not

translated into action?

—MAHATMA GANDHI

Where do you begin? In what area are you committed to making a difference? Are you committed to making this planet clean and healthy? A man I know has a big dream of ensuring that the rain forest is still in existence when his children's children are grown. Maybe your interest is in the area of health and medicine. How about a cure for cancer or AIDS in your lifetime? Or maybe your dream—to have more breathable air—can encompass both health and environmental issues. Perhaps your contribution will be in the area of education or communications.

As I mentioned, my big dream is to change the way people think about dreams. I want people to stop thinking about dreams in the negative, that dreams are something they can't have. Instead, I want people to think, "Dream? By when?" and start applying dates to their dreams.

Whatever your big dream is, this is an opportunity for you to get into action on it. You might be asking what difference you can make if you're only one individual. The Real People stories in this chapter are about individuals and organizations that have made a major contribution to society. Among them is the story of Anselm, an ordinary man who made a big difference by touching many lives globally with the projects he produced. He was only one individual, but he had a unique and special dream: to end world hunger.

If you are not the kind of person who can start a Make-a-Wish Foundation, perhaps you can volunteer at such an organization. Look around. Start with what you're passionate about, what matters to you, what moves you. Talk with people who are already involved and learn how you can participate. Make a contribution; that's one way to dare to dream big. Make a promise and then take action to fulfill your promise; that's what your life is about.

We are not here to do what

has already been done.

—ROBERT HENRI

How can you get in action? Mark your calendar; talk to someone; listen for a request; ask how you can help. As you're watching television or reading the newspaper, notice what moves you, angers you, turns you on, and touches your heart. That's a good place to begin.

The critical thing is to begin. One thing will lead to another. You'll know when it feels right, and the personal feeling of satisfaction and fulfillment will be beyond description. Perhaps all we want from our lives is to make a difference. This is one way to do it: dare to dream big.

Dreams bigger than your life

start the same as all dreams.

Real People: OPRAH WINFREY

Last year I surveyed a thousand people, asking them to name big dreamers whom they admired. The number one choice by far was Oprah Winfrey. What is it about Oprah that we love so much?

Is it that her Angel Network, by raising over $3 million, will help pay college tuition for kids all over the country in addition to supporting numerous other projects?

Is it her book club, in which she demonstrates her strong belief that education is freedom? Is it her use of her television show to bring back the power, meaning, and joy of the written word? Is it that she stands proudly for what she believes in?

Last week in San Francisco, I had the pleasure of speaking to six thousand women at the Mayor's Summit. When Oprah crossed the stage an hour later, the room was transformed. We were up close and in person with an icon, a very human, kind, and generous icon. It's rare when a person can bring both together, and Oprah does it with style. I think what we love most about her is that she is real. She struggles with human frailties and emotions like the rest of us. But she courageously does it, every day in front of 20 million viewers.

Real People: ANSELM ROTHSCHILD

Anselm Rothschild, a personal friend, was committed to ending hunger in the world, and he dedicated his life to doing so. He chose to pursue his dream by composing music and producing events that promoted global peace and an end to hunger.

During the 1960s, Anselm organized the Freedom from Hunger Foundation's first walkathon, which became the prototype for fund-raising walkathons across the country. He didn't stop there, however. While Anselm had lots of credits and credentials, he is probably best remembered as the head writer and coordinating producer of the educational components of the *LiveAid* telecast. Anselm was a man who followed his dream. I speak about him in the past tense because, unfortunately, he died before he reached forty. But what a life he lived.

He was indeed an extraordinary man, and he wrote a wonderful song that sums up much of what I've said in this book. It's called "Remember to Remember."

Although he wasn't able to end world hunger by the time he died, his contribution made a specific and measurable difference to billions of people. Anselm's message raised awareness of the problem to a new level through *LiveAid,* which was broadcast to 160 countries.

REMEMBER TO REMEMBER

Remember to remember,
It will light your heart each day,
It will help you on your way,
And it's more than just a saying so you know.

Remember to remember,
That is all you have to do,
And the truth will see you through
Even when all has darkened around you.

Who you said you are was brighter than a star,
Even though your dreams were dashed and knocked about,
You were still that dream under everything you doubt.

Remember to remember
How you said you wanted to be;
It will set and keep you free;
It will heal your wounds, caress your face with love.

Remember to remember,
If it's all you ever do,
And the truth will see you through;
You will hear God sing to you forever.

Who you said you are was brighter than a star,
Even though your dreams were dashed and knocked about,
You were still that dream under everything you doubt.

Remember to remember,
If it's all you ever do,
And the truth will see you through;
You will hear God sing to you forever.

—ANSELM ROTHSCHILD, © 1989

Real People: THE VOLUNTEERS
OF THE MAKE-A-WISH FOUNDATION

The Make-a-Wish Foundation is a nonprofit volunteer organization whose sole aim is to grant the wishes of children under age eighteen who are suffering from life-threatening illnesses. The foundation was started in 1980 when a dying youngster's dream to become a state trooper was granted. Since then more than ten thousand children across the United States have had their dreams come true, thanks to the Make-a-Wish Foundation.

Ordinary people can launch dreams

bigger than themselves.

Granting a sick child's wish provides a joyful and meaningful experience that benefits both the child and the family. Whether a child wishes to ride in a hot-air balloon, visit a favorite sports hero, or go to Disney World, the Make-a-Wish Foundation does everything possible to ensure that the wish becomes a reality.

The foundation depends completely on financial donations and on its volunteers' contributions of time. Those who elect to give of their energy are remarkable individuals, making the dreams of ailing children come true while satisfying their own desire to make a difference.

CHAPTER 17

Preparing Your Own Dreams Come True Workbook

**Before everything else,
getting ready is the secret of success.**

—HENRY FORD

OVER THE YEARS, ONE OF THE most effective vehicles I've found to ensure getting what you want is to prepare your own Making Your Dreams Come True Workbook. You'll find a sample workbook at the end of this chapter. I've left it blank so you can use it to start your own. It will help you design and gain clarity on your most heartfelt dreams.

Don't worry about having enough time to develop your workbook; if you've progressed this far you've done a lot of the work already. Now it's a matter of setting it up in a way that will allow you to live your dream.

You don't have to start over; you can go back and copy the information you need from the Passion Pyramid and the notes you might have made while working through earlier chapters. Begin by filling out your life's purpose. Then write the dreams you're committed to accomplishing, and list the projects you've designed to fulfill that dream.

You will remember that, to simplify things and to make this process really clear, you chose one area on which to focus while going through this book. Now you have an opportunity to go back to all the dreams under each category, to list four or five different projects for each dream, with specific results. If you haven't listed more than four or five projects, you can list next to each project the strategies and steps you can use to accomplish them.

Your Dreams Come True Workbook

will help you to set things up

in a way that will allow you

to live in your dream.

If you have a lot of projects, you can break them down even further. Thus, your completed Dreams Come True Workbook will consist of one overview sheet that states your purpose and your dreams, a page for each dream and its projects, and individual project sheets, listing all your strategies and steps.

When you have completed that part of your workbook, go back through your strategies and steps and start to make notes in the margin about resources that are available to you. Maybe there's a project you're not clear about, one you can't exactly envision. Look for inspiration to clarify it. Perhaps you can see three movies in the next month that will spur creative ideas about how to accomplish that project. Even if you can't see it clearly yet, looking for inspiration is one way to be in action on a project that supports your purpose and your dream.

Your Dreams Come True Workbook can be designed into a simple three-ring binder or in a beautiful book. Break the workbook down into the various sections: the overview, your purpose, your dreams, your projects. Don't be rigid about your workbook, however. You may want to change its format as you go along. In any event, give yourself lots of room to expand. You will find that your initial projects turn into other projects—often more creative, challenging, and rewarding, and one opportunity will lead to another. You won't know at first all the avenues that will become open to you; that's part of the magic of this process.

It's essential that you keep using any tool that you develop for getting what you want. That's why your Dreams Come True Workbook needs to be tied to your calendar, whether you put a calendar in your workbook or use your workbook side by side with your existing appointment book. Keep your workbook someplace visible and easily accessible. Open it every day or schedule a little dream time. It's a way for you to reread your dream and reconnect to your commitment. The power in doing so is that your dream exists outside of your head as well as in it; what you want is all right in front of you. with lots of clarity and room for expansion.

Use your workbook also as a place to hold your resources. Buy the plastic sleeves available in office supply stores so that you can store news clippings or other loose materials. Establish sections in your workbook for dreams you haven't yet fully developed. For example, if you want to turn a hobby into a business,

Since the mind is a specific

biocomputer, it needs specific

instructions and directions. The

reason most people never reach their goals

is that they don't define them,

learn about them, or ever seriously consider

them as believable or achievable.

Winners can tell you

where they are going,

what they plan to do along the way,

and who will be sharing the

adventure with them.

—DENIS WAITLEY

create a "My Company" section. If you want more bartering relationships, develop a "Bartering" section. You'll be surprised at how quickly you'll start to fill in those pages.

In the financial area of my own workbook, I have sections for all the different ways that are available for me to make money: speaking, workshops, book sales, sale of other products and services, investments, and sponsorship opportunities. Your workbook, in the area of personal finances, might include insurance plans, stock investments, trust funds, retirement accounts, certificates of deposit, stocks and bonds, educational funds, and contributions. In any aspect of your life for which you have a project, look for ways to subdivide the components; when you do, you will find more areas of opportunity that support and reinforce you in reaching your dream.

Your Dreams Come True Workbook is

a way for you to reread your dream and

reconnect to your commitment.

Remember, the power of your workbook is that you will now have a place to hold your dreams. Don't be concerned that you don't know how you're going to accomplish it all or that you have blank pages; simply create the space and allow surprises and resources to show up.

Making Your
Dreams Come True
Workbook

YOUR NAME

WHAT IS YOUR DREAM
OR THE ESSENCE OF YOUR DREAM?

_____

_____

_____

_____

_____

_____

_____

WHAT DO YOU INTEND TO ACCOMPLISH
OR CREATE TODAY?

_____

_____

_____

_____

_____

_____

_____

LIST THREE MEMORIES OF PASSION

1. _____

_____

2. _____

_____

3. _____

_____

MY LIFE'S PURPOSE

Version #1

_____

_____

_____

_____

_____

Version #2 (Make this easy to recall.)

_____

_____

_____

_____

_____

DREAM AREAS TO EXPLORE

Personal: _____

_____

_____

Professional: _____

_____

_____

Relationships: _____

_____

_____

Well-Being: _____

_____

_____

Financial: _____

_____

_____

Fun: _____

_____

_____

Other or Outrageous: _____

_____

CHECKPOINTS

Does each dream arise from your purpose?   Yes ____   No ____

Does it line up?   Yes ____   No ____

Does this dream turn you on?   Yes ____   No ____

Are you passionate about the   Yes ____   No ____
possibility this dream presents?

If you answered no, change your dream.

Pick a Life Area (personal, professional, etc.):

_____

_____

Dream:

_____

_____

	Projects	Key
1.	_____	____
2.	_____	____
3.	_____	____
4.	_____	____
5.	_____	____

Key

B - Being   S - Schedule   P - Plan   D - Done

MY DREAM, ASSUMING UNLIMITED RESOURCES

Describe your dream: _____

_____

Some areas to consider include: _____

_____

What are you doing? _____

_____

Where are you doing it? _____

_____

How do you feel? _____

_____

How do you look? _____

_____

Who are you with? _____

_____

What are you creating or accomplishing? _____

_____

Give some detail. _____

_____

_____

CHANGING YOUR BELIEF

My limiting belief that is stopping me from having my dream come true is _____

_____

_____

_____

_____

_____

_____

_____

My wonderful new belief is _____

_____

_____

_____

_____

_____

_____

_____

Choose which you will believe.

MY DREAM—VERSION #2

Now what's possible? _____

_____

_____

_____

_____

_____

_____

Are you committed to having this dream come true?

Yes _____   No _____

Do you believe it's possible?

Yes _____   No _____

If you answered yes, go on; if you answered no,
go back to "Changing Your Belief."

FROM DREAM TO PROJECT
OR FROM DREAM TO REALITY

What project can you create that represents your dream or will get you going on it? A project needs to be specific, measurable, and have a completion date. I recommend projects that can be done in three months or less.

Hint: You may simply add a date to your dream from the previous page.

Project: _____

_____

_____

_____

_____

_____

_____

_____

_____

_____

STRATEGIES AND STEPS
A ROAD MAP FOR GETTING THERE

Strategies:

1. _____

2. _____

3. _____

4. _____

5. _____

6. _____

For Strategy #_____, above, here are the steps ("to do" items) that I've chosen:

Date _____   Item _____   Resource _____

Date _____   Item _____   Resource _____

Date _____   Item _____   Resource _____

Date _____   Item _____   Resource _____

Date _____   Item _____   Resource _____

Date _____   Item _____   Resource _____

RESOURCES: THINGS I CAN DO
TO HELP MAKE MY DREAM COME TRUE

Places I can go: _____

_____

_____

_____

Things I can read: _____

_____

_____

_____

New things I can try: _____

_____

_____

_____

Old things I can reference: _____

_____

_____

_____

Where is the one place I know I can't get any help? _____

_____

_____

_____

How can I use this? _____

_____

_____

_____

RESOURCES: PEOPLE

Friends who can help me: _____

_____

_____

Friends of friends who can help me: _____

_____

_____

Family members who can help me: _____

_____

_____

Business associates who can help me: _____

_____

_____

Organizations and associations that can help me: _____

_____

_____

Who will support me? _____

_____

_____

Who can advise me? _____

_____

_____

Who can really help me? _____

_____

_____

People I don't know who can help me: _____

_____

_____

Who is the one person I won't get any help from? _____

_____

_____

How can I use even this? _____

_____

_____

_____

_____

_____

SCHEDULING

Put the "to do" items in chronological order and transfer them to your calendar.

Month _____

Day _____ To do _____

_____   _____

_____   _____

_____   _____

_____   _____

Month _____

Day _____ To do _____

_____   _____

_____   _____

_____   _____

_____   _____

Month _____

Day _____ To do _____

_____   _____

_____   _____

_____   _____

_____   _____

PASSION SCALE

Place an X next to the term that best describes your level of
passion.

_____ Red hot
_____ Turned on
_____ Excited
_____ Very interested
_____ Interested
_____ Some possibility
_____ No interest

CHAPTER 18

Epilogue:
The Beginning

We can create and live the life of our dreams.
Wake up and dream.

—MARCIA WIEDER

ALTHOUGH THIS IS THE LAST CHAPTER in the book, it is only the beginning for you. Remember that your dreams are the expression of your heart and soul. Get in touch with what matters most to you. Bring more of who and what you love into your everyday life. This is your life and although life is short, the way we live it, each and every day, can make it joyful and fulfilling. Remember the formula for making your dreams come true:

1. Get clear about what you want to create.
2. Remove the obstacles.
3. Design the simple steps to make your dream happen.

And remember to share your dreams with others. Build a DreamTeam. Ask people to join your team and ask how you can help them achieve their dreams.

Standing in your purpose and moving up the Passion Pyramid, you can see your dreams with crystal clarity and commit to having them. Use your resources—the ones you know about right now and the ones you can make available to yourself. Allow yourself to be imaginative and inventive, to create projects that will move you forward.

Design your internal and external environment so that it will nurture your dreams and the projects that will make your dreams come true. Trust the process, the synchronicity in the universe, and, most of all, yourself. You are, and you can be, as imaginative and resourceful as you need to be; get in action to live the life you love. Remember, you are a dreamer at heart.

Sharing your dream with others will help you enroll people to contribute time and energy to fulfilling your dream. When you can envision it in its entirety, you will be able to speak about your dream in a way that generates excitement and enthusiasm. The eagerness you engender in others will come back to you a thousandfold in heightened motivation to make your dreams come true.

Be unstoppable. You can have the life you want, the one that works for you. The possibilities are all waiting for you to let them happen, to produce extraordinary results, to make your life the magical experience it was meant to be.

Glossary

USEFUL WORDS FOR MAKING YOUR DREAMS COME TRUE

To speak of "mere words"
is much like speaking of "mere dynamite."

—C. J. DUCASSE

THE FOLLOWING WORDS ARE USED often by people who have made their dreams come true. You can use them in speaking your dream. Hear yourself use them and know yourself as a dreamer.

Accomplishment. Something you have done, succeeded in, or completed.

Acknowledge. To recognize or to express thanks for, to affirm.

Act. To move from one point to another; to be in motion; to move forward.

Alignment. When everything is arranged in a way that works and supports the whole.

Balance. Equal on all sides; the outcome is a sense of well-being and ease.

Belief. An assumption you have; a way of looking at things that determines your choices.

Clarity. Focus; a clear way of seeing something.

Coach. A person who is committed to your being a champion.

Completion. When something is whole; has integrity; all the pieces are there.

Conversation. A way of communicating and interacting with another person.

Design. To make something happen intentionally.

Devise. To plan; a plan of action.

Dream. A fond hope and a plan for accomplishing it.

Dream architect. Someone who helps other people accomplish their dreams by helping them get clear about what they want, by helping them to design a blueprint for achieving their dreams.

Dynamic. An energetic force that is intense, exuberant, unstoppable, in motion, full speed ahead, moving forward.

Energy. A force; a potential; the ability to move.

Enrollment. Sharing your dream in such a way that other people get excited.

Expressing. A way of communicating; conversing, relating, telling, declaring, imparting information to others.

Focus. An ability to see things clearly using different perspectives.

Fun. Amusement, mirth, gaiety.

Happiness. Enjoyment, pleasure, feeling good.

Harmony. When all things work together in unison.

Intention. Focus; direction.

Love. A way of being; that which has deep meaning and significance for you.

Measurable. Capable of being evaluated using specific criteria.

Movement. Relocation of something from one place to another.

Opportunities. The variety of ways of accomplishing something.

Participation. Involvement; making something happen.

Partnership. Relationships with people who can help you make your dreams come true.

Passion. Feeling turned on, energized, excited, enthusiastic; going full out, aligning mind, body, heart.

Play. To engage in, undertake, perform.

Possibility. The belief that anything and everything can happen; a powerful force.

Power. A form of energy, such as owning your own power; also a form of empowerment.

Projects. A unit of measure for accomplishing something; an accomplishment with a specific, measurable result; the way to bring your dreams into tangible form.

Purpose. Who you are in the world; work that you have chosen to do in the world; where passion comes from; what turns you on.

Relationships. A way of being with another person or other people or things.

Resources. Tools that are available to help you make your dreams come true, including people, places, things, and you.

Result. An accomplishment; something complete and whole that stands alone; something that can be identified and measured.

Schedule. To put something on your calendar; to assign a date by which something will happen.

Scheme. A plan of action.

Specific. An individual unit that is identifiable in time and space.

Step. That which moves you forward.

Strategy. A way of doing something; the how of getting something accomplished.

Success. A self-defined way of being, the outcome of which is a feeling of joy.

Tactics. The specific items to get you into action on making your dream come true.

Unlimited. No restrictions or limitations on what you want to accomplish.

Unstoppable. To keep going, no matter what happens.

Values. A way of being; a way of living your life.

Vision. A clear picture of what you want to accomplish or create.

Vitality. A level of energy and usefulness that one may have when living life on purpose.

Way of being. The expression of someone living a life in passion.

Way of living. Unlimited; no restrictions; anything goes.

Whole. Something that is, or someone who is, complete and intact and has all the pieces.

Work. An expression of who you are in the world.

About the Author

MARCIA WIEDER is known as America's Dream Coach. She is a top-rated presenter on visionary thinking, goal achievement, productivity, and team building to companies such as AT&T, Charles Schwab, American Express, The Gap, the Young Presidents' Organization, and many direct-selling companies.

She has written two other books, *Life Is But a Dream* and *Doing Less and Having More,* and produced an audiotape series called *Yes You Can . . . Make Your Dreams Real.* She has spoken to audiences all over the world, including thousands of kids.

She leads Dream University®, her weeklong program on passion and discovering your purpose. She has appeared on *Oprah* and *The Today Show* and has been featured in a national PBS television special entitled *Making Your Dreams Come True.*

Marcia is a former president of the National Association of Women Business Owners. She is the recipient of the Small Business Administration's Women in Business Advocate of the Year, and the Chivas Regal Entrepreneur of the Year Award.

She lives in her dream city of San Francisco, where she is pursuing her dream of living near the water and balancing work and play, with much more emphasis on play.

Register your dream on Marcia's Website:
www.marciaw.com

Marcia Wieder,
Motivational Speaker

MARCIA GIVES SPEECHES AND PRESENTS inspiring workshops
on dream achievement, team building, and visionary thinking.
She is known for her live-on-the-spot dream coaching of audiences from 50 to 5,000.

SPEECHES AND WORKSHOPS:

Igniting Passion in Your Work and Life
A Winning DreamTeam
Mapping Your Leadership Vision
Passion and Productivity
The Business of Making Dreams Come True
Dream University®

If you would like to know more about these or other workshops, please call 800-869-9881 or 415-433-9552
or visit Marcia's Website: www.marciaw.com

Marcia Wieder's
Dream University®

DREAM UNIVERSITY® IS A RARE opportunity to study with
Marcia Wieder in an intimate and small group workshop. This curriculum provides the structure to design a dream-come-true life.
By reclaiming your heart and soul, you will deepen your self-trust
and emerge as a very different person.

Marcia offers concrete principals balanced with experiential
exercises that are fun and practical. Work in depth with her five-
step technology: *Purpose, Dreams, Beliefs, Projects,* and *Teams,* for
easily getting what you want. Some exercises include story
telling, voice dialoging with your dreamer and doubter, a trust
walk on the land, and gathering in a dream circle to share the
wisdom learned.

In beautiful surroundings, learn the art of manifestation
from an expert. Use this retreat to recharge and regenerate, and
to learn to dream again. Each day begins with movement such
as stretching or walking. You will be introduced to different
ways to relax your body and mind, to access insight and intuition. Followed by breakfast, there is a morning session. Lunch
is bountiful, and most afternoons include ample free time for
exploring the land, swimming, having a massage, and to integrate what you are learning about being a dreamer. Reconvene
for a potent session before dinner, and end with an inspiring
evening program.

Dream University® is for you if:

➤ You want to create and realize an important personal or professional dream.

➤ You desire new clarity and resources for the twenty-first century.

➤ You want to express your voice as a visionary or leader.

➤ You dare to dream big!

This curriculum will:

➤ Offer a process for connecting to your life's purpose, providing renewed passion, vitality, and enthusiasm.

➤ Help you decide what really matters to you and what you will do about it.

➤ Reveal how you sabotage your dreams and teach you how to remove obstacles.

➤ Teach you how to build and inspire a DreamTeam.

For information or to register
call 800-869-9881 or 415-433-9552
Or visit www.dreamuniversity.com

A special audiotape series
YES YOU CAN . . . MAKE YOUR DREAMS REAL!
with America's Dream Coach, Marcia Wieder

➤Gain Clarity About What You Want
➤Remove Any And All Obstacles
➤Get "Into Action" On The Dreams That Matter To You

VOLUME I—BEGIN THE PROCESS
Tape One—Ignite Your Passion   Tape Two—The Dream Formula

VOLUME II—GET WHAT YOU WANT
Tape Three—Overcome Limits   Tape Four—Move Your Dream Forward

VOLUME III—DREAM COACHING: LIVING ON PURPOSE
Tape Five—Discover Your Dream   Tape Six—Dealing with Doubt

VOLUME IV—DREAM COACHING: FREE YOUR DREAMS
Tape Seven—Working Your Dream   Tape Eight—Dreams and Money

Entire 8-tape library: $79.00 including shipping

Name _____ Phone _____

Address _____

City _____ State _____ Zip _____

Credit card (MasterCard, VISA, American Express)

_____ Expiration date _____

Signature _____

Amount paid _____

Order by fax 415-433-6061, mail, or by visiting Marcia's Website
www.marciaw.com

Make check payable to:
Marcia Wieder, PMB 355, 110 Pacific Avenue, San Francisco, CA 94111